LAST BRIDGE to NOWHERE

J. FRANK PREWITT

PO Box 221974 Anchorage, Alaska 99522-1974
books@publicationconsultants.com—www.publicationconsultants.com

ISBN 978-1-59433-086-5
Library of Congress Catalog Card Number: 2008934406

Cover design by T. James Design

Manufactured in the United States of America.

Dedication

To my wonderful wife, Vicki, the gang at Nuts Landing, and our Kelly Jo.

Author's Note

My code name is Patient and I'm the confidential source the FBI relied on to expose the intricate web of political corruption chronicled in these chapters.

This book is based on hundreds of hours of undercover meetings with *perps* and other *persons of interest* to the FBI, conversations with agents and attorneys in the U.S. Department of Justice, secret recordings, transcripts and public records. This is my journal.

While care has been taken to protect the integrity of ongoing investigations, the people, events, and setting are real. The dialogue is transcribed, best recollection, or reasonable inference. The creative context is carefully researched to foster deeper understanding of the issues, characters and setting. Hang on; fiction just doesn't get this good.

Perps and Persons of Interest

United States Congress

- Sen Ted Stevens (R) *Senior member of Congress; Senate Appropriations Chair; President of Senate Pro Tempore*

- Rep Don Young (R) *Resources and Transportation Chair and seventh ranking member of the House of Representatives.*

Alaska Executive Branch

- Frank Murkowski (R) *former Governor and U. S. Senator of the State of Alaska*

- Jim Clark (R) *Chief of Staff to Governor Frank Murkowski*

Alaska Legislature

- Sen Ben Stevens (R) *Former Alaska Senate President; son of Ted Stevens*

- Sen John Cowdery (R) *Senate Rules Chair*

- Sen Jerry Ward (R) *Former Senate Finance*

- Sen Don Olson (D) *Chair Community and Regional Affairs; Senate Finance*

- Rep Tom Anderson (R) *Former House Judiciary Co-chair; former HSS Co-chair*

- Rep Pete Kott (R) *Former House Speaker*

- Rep Vic Kohring (R) *Former Chair House Oil & Gas*

•Rep Bruce Wehyrauch (R) *Former Chair House State Affairs*

•Rep Beverly Masek (R) *Former Representative*

Oil Industry Executives

•Bill Allen President and CEO VECO Intl. Inc. (acquired by CH2M Hill)

•Pete Leathard Vice President Operations VECO Intl Inc

•Roger Chan CFO VECO Intl. Inc.

•Rick Smith Vice President Government Affairs VECO Intl. Inc.

U.S. Department of Justice

•Lead Special Agent Mary Beth Kepner Anchorage FBI

•Special Agent Chad Joy Anchorage FBI

•Lead U.S. Attorney Nicholas Marsh, Public Integrity Unit, Washington DC

•Lead U.S. Attorney Joseph Bottini, Anchorage

Other

•Perry Green: businessman

•William C. Weimar: businessman

•William Bobrick: lobbyist

Contents

Indictment Transcript

Suite 604 Baranof Hotel
Juneau, Alaska
May 7, 2006

Representative Pete Kott: "I had to 'get 'er done;' I knew I had to come back and face you. I had to *cheat, steal,* beg, borrow, and *lie.*"

VECO CEO Bill Allen: "I own yer ass."

www.veco.com

Our Core Values
"Honesty: We maintain integrity by always matching our actions with our words. *We don't lie. We don't cheat. We don't steal.*"

Introduction
April 19, 2004

"Hang on a minute, would ya?" I slipped my headphone off as the racket of skidding gravel stopped and an ominous cloud of dust drifted past my window. As I peered out, the tight parking area in front of my house looked like a used car lot at year-end clearance. And pouring out of the dusty fleet of monotonous vans and sedans were a dozen or so equally nondescript suits and slacks, except for one thing, they had guns.

Lunging for the phone I yelled, "Get back to you later!" and stumbled my way through barking dogs clawing their way to the pounding at the door. I grabbed the dogs in one hand, my composure in the other, and opened the door to a serious woman holding a black wallet with her picture and badge.

"I'm Special Agent Mary Beth Kepner, FBI," she said. "May I speak with you?" The door pressed against my grip as a crowd of faceless, rubber-gloved coveralls swarmed past my dazed vision.

"Sure, what's up?" I answered.

What's up is one of the biggest cases of political corruption in United States history, that is, if you consider third chair to the President of the United States, a senior U.S. congressman, several aides, a dozen past and sitting state legislators, a few lobbyists, a prominent governor's chief of staff and the entire executive team of a major international oil service firm big fish. But I'm getting ahead of the story.

Chapter One
Confidential Source

Prisons are dirty business. A lot of the people who live there aren't very nice. Some of the people who work there aren't very nice either, and they cost a lot of money to run, money most people would rather spend on health, energy, education, and potholes. Unions can be dirty business. And some of the people who run them aren't very nice, particularly when they control a monopoly and someone threatens to break into the game. But when government unions and venture capitalists compete to run prisons, let's just say the line between the good guys and the bad guys can get, well, a bit fuzzy, *and that's how it all started.*

I'm CS-1, a recovering lawyer, bureaucrat, consultant, lobbyist, and FBI confidential source—respected enterprises with high ratings in the court of public opinion. As a bureaucrat I served as an assistant attorney general, deputy commissioner and commissioner of the State of Alaska Department of Corrections. As Confidential Source One, I offer strategic advice, wear a wire, record conversations, take pictures, and hang out with perps and persons of interest. Now why would a rational husband, father, and professional seek out such an enterprise? I didn't. Let's just say the FBI has inordinate powers of persuasion. But we'll get to that soon enough.

Alaska's an extraordinary place. Where else would people choose to locate their capital 600 miles from ninety five percent of the population in a place accessible only by air and sea, on a good day? Where else would people risk relying on oil taxes and royalties, largely controlled by the United Arab Emirates and international oil producers, to fund ninety nine percent of government operations? Where else would enterprising entrepreneurs turn moose crap (cleverly marketed as *nuggets*) into jewelry, Christmas ornaments, and tourist trinkets? By 2003 this unusual compost of big oil, frontier ingenuity, and isolated lawmaking reached critical mass, seeping lethally into the cracks and crevices of Alaska public policy and under the door of FBI Special Agent Mary Beth Kepner.

The catalyst for corruption had been twenty years in the making. It began in the mid '80s when the trans-Alaska pipeline bonanza was just a nostalgic memory triggered by occasional sightings of tattered bumper stickers pleading, *"God, please give us another pipeline and I promise not to piss it away this time."* In the aftermath of an unprecedented wave of prosperity, the post-Alaska pipeline economy adjusted like a retreating tsunami, leaving much of Alaska strangling in the backwash of bankruptcy, foreclosures, declining revenue, and shrinking population. To make matters worse, economists warned of a gradual, but imminent decline in oil production and corresponding budget deficits of mindwrenching proportions.

But with all the doom and gloom, there was one bright spot in the economy. As the result of 1978 justice *reforms,* mid-'80s Alaska distinguished itself with one of the highest per capita incarceration rates in the free world, stimulating the economy with high-paying prison construction jobs and stable employment in a new growth industry. In less than a decade (with a little nudge from a successful prisoner rights lawsuit), Alaska's tiny network of provincial jails evolved from a footnote agency of Health and Social Services into one of the biggest departments of State government, hosting, to this day, Alaska's largest organized group of public employees: *correctional officers,* an affiliation of public servants who, compared to other government union workers, wield grossly disproportionate leverage over their own wages and benefits.

Operating behind razor-wire fences, bars, and concrete, the society of corrections controls or repels meaningful public access to its world by relying on the sacred mantra, "concern for safety and internal security." Controlling access to information enables Corrections to define its own truth about incidents, safety, security, conditions and needs. This comes in handy when Corrections officials hand the legislature the department's annual bill for operations. But it's particularly handy just before correctional officer union contract negotiations, when grave public safety concerns over executive-level mismanagement, staffing shortages, low pay, internal working conditions, and the sacrifice of public service are reluctantly shared through discreet venues such as press conferences, rallies, and sensational prime-time advertising.

Anchorage Daily News
04/23/08
By Megan Holland

NO CONFIDENCE VOTE CENSURES STATE PRISON BOSS

Tensions escalated in the state's prisons Tuesday with corrections officers publicly censoring their boss. The workers, through their union, gave Commissioner Joe Schmidt a "vote of no confidence," which passed 514 – 19. Members of the union, the Alaska Correctional Officers Association, allege that Schmidt has cut staff to dangerous levels. Schmidt said the allegations by the union are false and the union was looking to unsettle him in future contract negotiations. (Ah, some things never change.)

The Alaska Correctional Officers Association's inordinate leverage is the result of geographic isolation and Alaska's *unified* system of corrections, a state constitutional anomaly which systemically has more in common with authoritarian than with democratic forms of government. With the exception of Federal Probation and Parole, in Alaska the state manages all prison, jail, halfway house, probation, and parole services. In other states offenders are parceled between city, state, county, and federal correctional agencies, depending on the jurisdiction and gravity of the offense. Like in the free marketplace, competing government agencies within the borders of a given state act as a check and balance on employee wages and benefits. In other words, pay in one agency in one jurisdiction is comparable to similar work in another. But Alaska's post territorial correctional system fostered the creation of a disproportionately large, single class of government employees who, through mystery and solidarity, were able to muscle their way out of general employee bargaining units and into their own powerful union. Don't get me wrong. I am not at all opposed to unions and appreciate the protections they afford workers. It's monopolies I oppose.

Over the years, the absence of competition in Alaska corrections (multiple jurisdictions, if you prefer) has created a government oligarchy that drives the cost of managing prisons and jails in Alaska to double and triple the cost of similar services in comparable communities, gracing Alaska with the world's most expensive correctional system. At a combined average capital and operating cost of more than one hundred fifty dollars per inmate, per day, one would think that the only things lacking in Alaska's prisons are room service and heated towels. But one would be wrong.

Armed with a high school diploma and 6 weeks of training, in the late '80s and early '90s Alaska's elite *Tier One* guards entered the workforce paid double the industry norm for week-on/week-off shifts, in a twenty-year full retirement plan with built-in overtime and geographic pay incentives. In the early '90s Alaskan guards with seventeen years of service flocked to rural Alaska communities where they could retire after their *three high years of service* on a base annual salary approaching one hundred thousand dollars, give or take pocket change. Most are now retired, or quietly retiring, in nests feathered by the misguided fiscal policies of an oil boom economy.

Needless to say, the golden retirement parachute eliminated any illusion of local hire in rural Alaska's Native communities, where Corrections is often the largest employer. But that little problem is mitigated by an extraordinary affirmative action partnership between the State of Alaska and her indigenous peoples. Eskimo, Aleut, and Indian Alaskans share in the economic stimulus of prison expansion through public policies that induce Native men to occupy nearly forty percent of the beds in Alaska's prisons and jails. With the highest proportional incarceration rate of First Peoples in North America, three percent of Alaska's general population, or Native men over eighteen, occupy nearly forty percent of the prison and jail beds, a travesty of monumental proportions (but that's another story).

By the mid '90s, self-corrective forces were at work. Oil at nine dollars per barrel, a nine hundred million dollar projected budget deficit, inflated prison costs, and an eight to ten percent annual offender growth rate combined to create *a perfect storm* of opportunity for the private sector. Faced with unconstitutional levels of prison overcrowding, desperate Alaska policymakers soon discovered comparable correctional services at half the cost in privately operated facilities in and outside the state of Alaska. They also discovered that felons, misdemeanants, and parking law scofflaws were all housed in the same facilities. So, from 1993 to 1995, hundreds of low-risk prisoners were transferred from state prisons and jails to private halfway houses, and the overflow of high-risk prisoners to a privately owned and operated prison in Arizona, at a fraction of the cost of in-state incarceration. In 1998, after three successful years of outsourcing prisoner supervision, the Alaska Legislature backed a private venture to build and operate a private prison in Alaska. The State Corrections Union had finally priced itself out of the market-place.

The union monopoly was now in serious jeopardy and the stakes were worth millions of dollars in cash and benefits. For some, all bets on propriety, fair play, honor, and rule of law were off, and no one at the table was going to fold. But who knew then that the struggle over establishing a private prison in Alaska would uncover an unprecedented culture of state and national political corruption far removed from the petty tug-of-war over who supervises the people we choose to separate from our midst.

"Any guns in the house?" said an intense guy with a crew cut standing next to Kepner.

"Uh, yeah. My father-in-law has a couple in his apartment. He's in his seventies, I think he's down at the Senior Center. I have a loaded Colt .357 in my upper right-hand desk drawer."

Crew cut walked away and Kepner said, "Frank, where can we talk?"

I said I needed to see my wife and we walked into the living room where *crew cut* was sitting on a couch asking her questions. I walked over and told him that this was about me, not Vicki, and to leave her alone. He got up and found something else to do. She looked up and appealed to me through frightened, tear-filled eyes, and I assured her everything would be fine, or so I thought.

We left the living room and walked by my office, where rubber-gloved coveralls were rifling through drawers and files, fiddling with my computer and loading things into boxes. I led Kepner and another suit to my father-in-law's little apartment and we sat facing each other. Kepner handed me a document. The upper right corner of the top page said *Search Warrant*. Time froze for a surreal moment as my eyes ricocheted from bold font to fine print, unable to settle on any combination of words that made any sense: *United States District Court - Case Number Anc1504 - any Authorized Officer of the United States - In the Matter of the Search of...Wait! That's my name!*

Kepner said they were there to collect any records of meetings, conversations, communications, contacts, bank statements, campaign contributions, or anything else concerning the initiative to establish a private prison in Alaska, and any of the people involved.

"Am I under arrest?" I asked.

"No," she replied, "but we're real interested in talking to you."

I suggested all she had to do was ask, but Kepner looked me in the eyes and said, "We didn't know whether you'd help and couldn't risk you destroying evidence."

"Evidence of what?" I asked.

"Evidence that your clients have been buying elected officials, for a start," she replied.

"And if I refuse to help?"

Kepner calmly answered, "Do you remember Don Stohlworthy?"

I thought for a moment and said, "Okay, tell me when and where you want to meet."

I first met Stohlworthy in the early '90s. Nixon's former Interior Secretary, the visionary Walter Hickel, had just been elected Governor of Alaska for the second time after a clever, last-minute bait-and-switch conversion from Republican to Independent. After the election, of course, the apostate Hickel converted back to Republican and all was forgiven—well, perhaps not by Arlis Sturgelewski, the Republican frontrunner he had stolen the election from, but by most everyone else. Stohlworthy was one of Hickel's political groupies. A staunchly conservative, butch-cut opportunist, Stohlworthy bounced around from assignment to assignment giving Hickel's chiefs-of-staff and press secretary ulcers and sleepless nights.

I didn't have much to do with Stohlworthy until I was appointed Hickel's prison czar. Since my office was in Anchorage and the governor's office was eight hundred miles away in Juneau, Hickel's chief of staff (a jolly guy named Pat Ryan) sent Stohlworthy up to see me with a note pinned to his collar that read *Deputy Commissioner*. I didn't take the hint, commended Ryan on his self-serving wit, and quickly filled the position with someone else. After one tumultuous term, a reluctant Hickel elected not to run again and I lost touch with Stohlworthy until 2002, when I learned he was a probation officer at the Anchorage jail and organizer of the *Corrections Officers for Murkowski* political action committee.

That was the year well-tenured Republican U.S. Senator Frank Murkowski decided to give up his seat in Washington DC and return to Alaska to run for governor against out-going Democrat Lite Governor Fran Ulmer. Since Stohlworthy was a conservative and the Corrections Officers union supported Democrats, he saw an opportunity to hedge bets by organizing a splinter group of Corrections employees to support Murkowski. Murkowski won the election and Stohlworthy was awarded the post of deputy commissioner of the Department of Corrections for his effort. This time he got a real badge, instead of a note pinned to his collar.

Before we move on, I think I mentioned that the State of Alaska passed legislation in the late '90s authorizing the construction of a privately managed prison in Alaska. Truth be told, the legislature passed four bills authorizing the same project in three different communities, over six successive years—and there are still no private prisons in Alaska. That should offer some insight into the magnitude of the government union versus private sector tug-of-war over who builds and runs prisons and jails in our country. It's just plain big business, worth millions of dollars to local economies in jobs, goods and services; worth millions to shareholders of private prison companies; and worth millions in influence, salaries, and benefits to government union employees.

The debate is actually quite simple: Private companies claim they can build and operate prisons for substantially less money than government without compromising service and safety. After all, guarding prisoners isn't brain surgery, even most hospitals (which do perform brain surgery) are privately built and operated. Government union opposition is, well, more philosophical. The unions believe taking care of prisoners is strictly a government function that shouldn't be outsourced to the corrupting influence of the market-place, because unions aren't motivated by money, uh, excuse me, profit.

But government unions and private corporations do have one thing in common. The bigger the corporation *or* union, the greater the influence over public policy, and in politics, influence is all about money. For private corporations, influence increases the bottom line for shareholders; for public unions, influence increases the wages and benefits of members; for elected officials, influence is about winning the next election, and all of that takes money—large amounts of money that changes hands, *and* expectations. There are rules of engagement, of course, rules that level the playing field. But when the stakes are high, who wants a level playing field?

The first private-prison bill in Alaska was a slam-dunk. The U.S. Department of Defense mothballed a military base along the Alaska Highway on the outskirts of a small community called Delta Junction. A re-use commission was appointed to find a use for the base that would backfill the devastating economic void left by the Army's departure. There were no takers, of course, so the community was delighted when a private consortium called Corrections Group North leased the base with a plan to build a prison.

The concept was simple and popular: Return Alaska's prisoners and jobs to Alaska by adding value to an abandoned military base, a win-win for the state and local economy, the federal government, the prisoners and their families. Why, it even won the support of victims' rights groups, who smiled at the thought of prisoners moving from sunny Arizona to Delta Junction, where the wind rarely drops below thirty five miles per hour and temperatures reach thirty degrees below zero, on a good day. The plan fizzled when the feds reclaimed the base facilities as an intercontinental missile site and Delta Junction backed out of its contract with the prison developer. It seems newly elected Mayor Roy Gilbertson found being *ground zero* for a nuclear or terrorist attack more appealing than living near a medium security prison. Go figure.

When the Delta Junction project skidded sideways, the same developers were approached by the Alaska Kenai Native Association to build and operate a prison on their land and to lobby the legislature to amend the enabling legislation. One of the reasons the Delta legislation went so smoothly is that the two dominant government unions were occupied in a turf war over who would represent the state's one thousand correctional officers. The unions were still mud wrestling when the Legislature amended the Delta Junction bill to allow the Kenai Peninsula Borough to lease the prison, hire a private contractor to run it, and sell the services to the state.

In a serious game of catch-up bankrolled by the California Corrections Officers Union, Alaska prison guards organized and successfully pressed for a borough wide referendum to approve or disallow the prison. With an army of correctional foot soldiers, one hundred fifty thousand dollars worth of direct mail, and fright commercials about escapees raping and plundering their way through defenseless Alaska communities, the unions handed the private developers their hats in a resounding defeat at the polls.

Within days the private prison developers were contacted by three other Alaska cities interested in the prison. Two and a half million development dollars in the hole and smarting from the Delta Junction and Kenai losses, the investors reluctantly agreed to take one final shot with the City of Whittier, a cold and windy seaport less than an hour south of Anchorage by highway. Why? It was an election year, and the polls showed that U.S. Senator Frank Murkowski was a shoo-in to win the Alaska race for governor. Surely a Republican Legislature and a Washington DC savvy Republican Governor would show the unions the door.

Governor's Conference Room - January 2004

Present: Governor Murkowski Chief of Staff Jim Clark; Office of Management and Budget Director Cheryl Frasca; Corrections Commissioner Mark Antrim; Corrections Deputy Commissioner Portia Babcock-Parker; Representative Mike Hawker; Frank Prewitt and others from the private prison development team.

The governor's conference room in Anchorage is a square, beige, functional space just large enough to seat people in chairs against the wall a couple of feet behind those seated at the conference table. The governor's chief of staff, Jim Clark, entered as we were standing around making polite small talk. A courteous tension spiced the generally boring bureaucratic atmosphere of the room. Clark asked us to be seated and introduced his staff and a few of the more distinguished luminaries at the table, such as Mark Pfeffer, the Governor's former campaign chair and major contributor (who was also an architect on the private prison design team), Representative Mike Hawker and the development team lobbyists. Clark ignored the current and former commissioners of Corrections.

Clark proceeded, "It's January 2004 and the private/public prison debate, or should I say debacle, has been going on for six years." Glaring at the lobbyists and me, he continued, "We proposed a state-built and state-operated prison north of Anchorage last year and you and your friends in the legislature killed it. You introduced a plan to build a privately operated prison at Whittier and we killed it. The governor instructed me to meet with you today to work out a compromise."

In about an hour there was consensus that the details of the compromise would be hammered out between Deputy Commissioner Stohlworthy and the lead consultant and spokesman for the private prison consortium, me. *Great* I mumbled. *Stohlworthy.* The two lobbyists chuckled. They knew Stohlworthy from the Hickel years. Concentrating on Clark and trying to keep a straight face, I heard an unidentified voice behind me whisper, "Remember, Grasshopper, compromise makes a good umbrella, but a poor roof." Without turning I nodded deeply and whispered, "Thank you, Great One," and left the room wondering who made the crack and whether he was serious. No one could have suspected that four years later the same Jim Clark would plead guilty to charges of public corruption and face a five year sentence to federal prison.

In a week or so I got a call from Stohlworthy. "I'll be in Anchorage next week. How about eleven thirty a.m. lunch on Wednesday at the Sea Galley on C Street?" he asked.

"Sounds great. See you there," I replied, and thought to myself, "Ah, Sea Galley, Anchorage cuisine at its finest. An *outside* (see Glossary) restaurant chain doing business in Alaska serv'n up Loosiana shrimp, 'Lantic cod, pathetic Argentine farm salmon and skinny crab legs from *Yuckitan* in the fresh seafood capital of the world! How Stohlworthy."

Don arrived punctually. The years since I had last seen him had served him well: same straight-back, crew cut, tight-assed guy I remembered, but with a new touch of arrogance, or maybe it was just the lighting. As we caught up, I softened a little as I listened to him recount his tough time finding employment after Hickel threw in the towel, his Wyoming sojourn, a divorce, his return to Alaska broke and the "dep com bone" he was thrown when *he* was the guy who got the guard union behind Murkowski.

After lunch we agreed to take a run to the proposed prison site and talk about the compromise legislation. It was nostril-hair-freezing cold out and Stohlworthy seemed singularly disinterested in the scenery or the site. He mostly spent the hour down and back telling me that, even though he was directed to work out a compromise plan, the personal fallout could be bad news. Over the highway drone he said, "Frank, what if Murkowski's a one-term governor? The unions will kill me if I'm the guy who drops a private prison on Alaska. Who's gonna take care of me?" He went on to suggest a variety of ways that might make him feel more comfortable making a positive recommendation about the prison, mostly guarantees of employment if he got fired or Murkowski lost the next election. Over weeks of phone calls and meetings, Stohlworthy's theme became increasingly less about building a compromise and more about what kind of assurances the private-prison principals could promise to guarantee his future financial security should the unions "take him out." And finally, he asked for money…a lot of it.

Back in my office and frustrated by the lack of progress, I said, "Don, can our guys offer you a position if you deliver this? No, they can't do that, it's illegal. But, if you're out front, the prison bill doesn't pass, and the unions get you fired, I'll start working the phones with, 'Hey this guy tried to help, let's try to find him something,' but Don, no one's going to do anything unethical or illegal. No one's going to offer you a job and no one is going to pay you a contingency fee. You need to open your eyes and make some calculated decisions."

———

At two p.m. the day after the FBI search, I met with Mike Spann, my attorney, and described the situation. Mike was a former U.S. Attorney well familiar with the patterns, practices, and eccentricities of the federal justice system. He said he'd give the U.S. Attorney's office a call and tell them we were willing to meet and talk after we saw the basis for their concern.

A couple of days later I got a phone call: "Frank?"

"Yeah Mike, what's up?"

"Hey, my man," he said, "Do you know a guy named Don Stohlworthy?"

I groaned, "Not him again."

Mike went on, "I'm looking at a transcript where he's pumping you for a job and money, and after a little dancing around, you tell him to pound sand. He was wearing a wire. The FBI says you bribed him with a job offer."

I shook my head in disbelief and said, "Right, I get it, they really do want to talk with me real bad. See if you can set up a meeting."

The morning of April 23, 2004, I sat in a small auditorium at the University of Alaska trying desperately to concentrate on my daughter's graduate degree dissertation. I don't remember her thesis. I do remember giving her a hug and trying to avoid her discerning eyes. We exchanged niceties and I escaped before she could ask me if something was wrong. I headed downtown, parked, plugged a meter, and walked across the street for a one-thirty p.m. meeting with my lawyer. At two p.m. he escorted me the short distance to the Federal Building. *Dead Man Walking* came to mind, but I shifted my attention to some plump ravens laughin' it up on a dumpster, scarfin' french fries and pointin' mocking black feather fingers my direction, or so it appeared.

At the Federal Building we emptied our pockets through several tiers of wand-waving security and approached a door with a camera peering down. The door lock snapped open and Special Agent Kepner appeared, motioning us to a small conference room where people were gathering. Introductions were made, we all sat down, I poured a glass of water, and the questions began.

At first the questions were general: "Tell us about yourself. Where'd you go to school? Been married before? What do you like to eat? Ever kick your dog? Why do you go by Frank when your name is James?" that sort of thing. I got the impression they were checking me out on the small things to see if I had a propensity to skirt the truth. The grunts and frowns also seemed to indicate that I didn't exactly square with their psychological profile (my wife says the same thing). We ended the *This Is Your Life* phase around five p.m. and Mike and I walked back to his office.

"So, how'd that go?" I asked. In his own colorful way Mike offered that today was just the tail sniffing stage. The real questions would come tomorrow.

We met again at nine a.m. the next day. The questions were more specific this time: "How feasible is the Whittier private prison proposal? Can you really build and operate it for less than the state? Isn't Whittier's infrastructure too small and isolated to support a project that big? Where are you going to find staff? How much are you really going to pay them? What happened at Delta Junction and Kenai? Why did you close the Wildwood Prison in 1993 when you were commissioner? What did you do with all of the prisoners? Tell us about Bill Weimar. When did you first meet him? How'd you convince Cornell Companies to buy his business? What do you know about his bankruptcy? Who put together his offshore trust? What do you know about his Seattle businesses?" Around three o'clock I was still busy answering questions when I saw Kepner lean toward one of the attorneys, whisper something and nod. I paused, she looked up, the room got stone quiet, and she asked, *Can you help us?*

What a strange question. I thought for a moment. Like pieces from a jigsaw, the two days of questions were taking the shape of an incredible picture, almost funny if it hadn't been about me. It seems corrections union sympathizers had fed the FBI a theory that I had conspired in 1993 to close state corrections facilities and dramatically increase the contracts of private corrections companies by moving offenders into privately owned and operated facilities. The alleged beneficiaries were Bill Weimar (who owned the lion's share of Alaska halfway houses), Cornell Companies (the private national corrections corporation that acquired Weimar's company), and Corrections Corporation of America (the company that supervised Alaska prisoners in Arizona). The *quid pro quo*, they theorized, was a lucrative consulting contract to broker the sale of Weimar's company to Cornell and create a private prison consortium to steal the Arizona contract by building and operating a private prison in Alaska, the latter requiring enabling legislation and an agreement with the state to purchase the new beds and services.

The theory wasn't bad, as theories go, because that was exactly what I was hired to do *after* I left government service. But the *quid pro quo* evaporated like a mirage after the Feds verified there was no basis for the allegation beyond competitive sour grapes. For fifteen years Weimar had outmaneuvered a succession of corrections administrators, strategically positioning himself as the sole beneficiary of escalating incarceration rates and declining government revenue, by purchasing and rezoning properties throughout the state to house low-risk offenders on the cheap.

From 1992 to 1995, the public record is replete with executive and legislative branch hand-wringing efforts to head off an impending fiscal crisis because of declining oil production and massive associated reduction in state revenue. But in an eighty five percent oil dependent state, there's only one place to cut expenses: the government operating budget, and cut they did. Yet even in the midst of extreme cuts to their own agencies, top cops, court system administrators, and justice professionals backed my repeated warnings to the governor and legislature that Corrections could not sustain budget cuts without closing facilities and releasing prisoners, or finding *less costly* alternatives to do business.

> Anchorage Daily News
> August 29, 1994
> Editorial
>
> Prison System Has No Choice
> It'd be nice to think Alaska's legislative leaders just don't get it. That way you could assume they were doing their best to balance the state prisons budget. Unfortunately that's not the way it is. When Corrections Commissioner Frank Prewitt said recently he is purposely overspending his budget to comply with court ordered restrictions on overcrowding, no one was surprised. Prewitt was blunt throughout the past legislative session...He told them again and again that he needed more money to run the prisons right. The Legislature responded by giving Corrections $3.3 million less than last year and $7.3 million less than what Prewitt said he needed this year.
>
> What legislators have done just plain stinks. They purposely shorted Corrections and ballyhooed their budget-cutting skills, then patted themselves on the back for passing a passel of crime bills that will lead to longer sentences and more prisoners.

And *less costly* Weimar smiled all the way to the bank.

Built on a false foundation, the conspiracy theory evaporated. The hypothesis, as I said, had Corrections Union fingerprints all over it, particularly in regard to small things like the truth and facts. But years earlier AFL-CIO's ever-umbrageous Greg O'Clary had warned that I'd never work in Alaska again if I continued to push government out-sourcing. I just naively thought my union friends wouldn't stoop to Chicago mob tactics.

That didn't mean Kepner's instincts were entirely off base. There were other reasons she was interested in Weimar and some of the other corporate prison development partners. I was their corrections consultant and Kepner figured I might have seen or heard things that could shed light on other concerns. By that time I was beginning to suspect her sights were set way too low, but neither of us could have foreseen the dramatic detour her concerns were about to take. Kepner was in unfamiliar terrain, yet she was on the right scent. All she needed was an experienced hunting partner.

So, what do you say, will you give us a hand? A now familiar voice pulled me to the surface of my mind. I looked at Kepner and said, "Let me talk it over with my attorney and I'll get back to you." Spann told me the best way to clear any remaining cloud over my name was to help the Feds determine which, if any, of their concerns had merit, and that would require signing a cooperation and confidentiality agreement. A few days later we shook hands and began an extensive debriefing. A few weeks later I got a call from Spann telling me the Feds were unusually delighted with my work. He said they agreed there was no basis for federal charges against me and I was under no obligation to continue helping, but they sure hoped that I would. I thanked Mike, hung up, dialed Kepner and offered to help in any way that I could. By that time I'd seen and heard enough to realize there was a pattern and practice of backroom politics in Alaska that had to stop. I knew the risk, but stepping out of the game wasn't an option, besides, it was just getting interesting.

I think, somehow Kepner knew all along that I'd agree to stay in for the long haul. Though at times I wonder what my new friends would have done to, shall we say, encourage my patriotism had I declined.

Chapter Two
Low Hanging Fruit

Political corruption cases can be very confusing. After the Confidential Source signing ceremony we all shook hands and agreed to work together to stomp out crime and crush the bad guys. I was assigned to Special Agent Kepner and my code name was *Patient*. She never said whether the name was due to my status or long-suffering nature, but there was no confusion over the anatomy under her control, when she said to turn my head and cough, I did.

Introduction into the Society of Confidential Sources equips one with a wide array of gifts and talents that I mostly can't talk about, you know, for your own security. But I was just learning how to operate my phone *device* when I got a call from my old friend Bill Weimar telling me that our old friend, former Senator Jerry Ward, who was running for reelection, was being bribed by Jim Clark, the governor's chief of staff, to drop out of the 2004 primary election.

I dropped the phone, scrambled to untangle the wires to my little silver box, stuck the combined receiver/transmitter in my ear and said, "Bill, sorry, I dropped the phone, what'd you say?" Bill said Ward received an offer from Clark, through Allen, to drop out of the state senate race. I said, "Bill Allen?"

Weimar replied, "Yeah, VECO Bill Allen told Ward that he would hire him for seventy thousand dollars between now and the end of the year and after that the governor would hire Ward and his wife into a couple of big-bucks state jobs until the end of his administration." I heard a muffled cough and Weimar continued, "He said Clark also agreed to settle Ward's wife's ten-year-old EEO claim against the State for one hundred thousand dollars, can you believe it!?"

"Yesss!" I thought, "I can believe it." I had told Kepner a week earlier she needed to keep the case covert as long as she could because there were fish out there that made Bill Weimar look like a minnow, and VECO Bill Allen was one of them. I wrapped up the call with Weimar and dialed Kepner's cell.

Suite 604 of the Juneau Baranof Hotel is affectionately known as the "Bill Allen Suite." Legislative staffers call it the *Animal House*. Allen was the CEO of VECO Corporation, an oil service company that employed over four thousand people worldwide and carried the major oil producers' political water. Allen also owned the conservative *Voice of the Times*, which held an editorial half page opposite the editorial page of Alaska's one major newspaper, the *Anchorage Daily News.* That was a deal made after the *Anchorage Times* lost a subscriber showdown with the *Daily News* many years before. Always fair and balanced, the *Voice of the Times* reserved plenty of ink for the oil and gas side of missiles fired from the opposing *progressive Daily News* editorial page.

State taxes and royalties on Alaska oil are a big deal to the state and the major oil producers. The formula for conflict doesn't take an economist to understand: more tax = less producer profit = more state revenue and less tax = more producer profit = less state revenue. In 2006 alone, the State of Alaska collected 3.4 billion dollars in oil money and bumped the oil driven Alaska Permanent Fund savings account to thirty three billion dollars. The stakes on even the minutest of regulatory adjustments are high, real high. And lobbyists, consultants, spinoff businesses, watchdog groups, investors, nonprofit beneficiaries (did I mention lawyers?), and an army of bureaucrats have made careers feeding off the crumbs of oil and gas related issues pending before Alaska's legislative and administrative bodies. And most of the action occurs in Alaska's quaint capital city of Juneau.

Downtown Juneau is about the size of a large casino. The legislature and governor's office are located in a six story brick building connected to a handful of offices, restaurants, bars, and cheesy hotels by semi-covered sidewalks, a practical amenity for a place with over one hundred inches of annual rain. Oil and gas legislation is a high-stakes game that opens in January each year, when the legislature convenes, and closes in May when the legislature adjourns. As in any casino, the games are played in a variety of places at all hours of the day and night. For two decades, Suite 604 had a running, invitation-only, high-stakes table hosted by oil exec Bill Allen and his vice president of Government Affairs, Rick Smith.

I had a membership in Suite 604 from 1998 to 2003 when VECO was the construction partner in the Corrections Group North private prison consortium. The construction arm of VECO specialized in horizontal, rather than vertical construction. That meant they'd never built a prison, or any other big building for that matter, but could probably figure it out. As Rick Smith said, "Cain't be much more compuhlcated then lay'n pipe, ken it?" But it really wasn't VECO's construction credentials the developers were after anyway; it was their remarkable access to key players in the legislature, governor's office and United States Congress, the go-to guys, Senator Ted "Earmark" Stevens and "Congressman For All Alaska (and Florida Coconut Road)" Don Young.

Union and press perception to the contrary, VECO didn't really do much to advance the prison cause. I'm sure a few doors opened, or votes went our way because of their influence, but the prison was pretty small potatoes, so VECO dropped out in 2003 to channel its energy and resources to an Alaska gas pipeline. But I did work with them long enough to make a few casual observations about Allen's and Smith's ready access to government policy makers, and concluded that it wasn't about charm and good looks, well, maybe a little charm.

Suite 604 occupies about eight hundred square feet of the southwest corner of the sixth floor of the Baranof Hotel. Just get off the elevator from the main lobby, take a right and knock on the door. Like a scene from an old James Cagney movie, the door opens a crack and a pair of bloodshot eyes scan the hallway.

"Hi, Rick." I said.

"Hey, pardner, what's up?"

"Just wondered whether you've heard how our bill is doing in House Finance?" I could hear laughter inside. Casually attired in plaid boxers, ball cap, and red-wine-stained Fruit-of-the-Loom tank top, Rick opened the door, yawned, scratched his butt, and led me down a hallway. I didn't really need a guide—all I had to do was follow my nose and burning eyes through the cigar smoke and stale whiskey permeating the air and my gasping pores.

"Frank!" a voice yelled through the whiskey-laden fog. "How in hell ya doin'? Pour yerself a drink o' the good shit. You like Silver Oak don'tcha?" Through the fog I could see Bill Allen pointing to a table with open bottles of wine, whiskey, gin, vodka, beer, tequila, and soda. In front of the booze was a mouthwatering presentation of gourmet canapés: Biscotti, Cheetos, Fritos, Sourcream Lays, and some Mother's healthy oatmeal cookies, which would have made their own quite proud, I'm sure. I poured a glass of Silver Oak and sat down next to Rick.

Across the room House Speaker Pete Kott held up a glass and asked how the prison was coming. I said it seemed to be going fine and he said to make sure to let him know if we needed any help. As I glanced around the room, four or five members of the Senate and House leadership were smoking cigars and watching a ball game replay on cable TV. Allen was deep in conversation with John Cowdery, the Senate Rules chair. It was midsession, the floor debates were over, and apparently the House and Senate had called it a day.

I chatted with Rick for a while and thought about the time I'd caught him and 'ol Bill with their proverbial pants down at VECO headquarters, the one in Anchorage, not Suite 604. I needed to talk to Rick about some benign issue and dropped in. The receptionist recognized me and said to go through the door on her left, down the hall, past the conference room, take a right and just knock on his door. Approaching the conference room, I heard Rick's voice and looked through the open door. Standing in front of a huge whiteboard, with that deer-in-the-headlights look, were Rick, Bill Allen, Senate President Rick Halford, and a handful of prominent Republicans. Behind them was a list of twenty or so mostly Republican legislators with four-and five-digit dollar figures next to their names. I told Rick I'd catch him later and moved on by.

Rick broke the daydream. "Don't worry, man, look around, the House Speaker, the Senate Majority Leader, the Senate Rules chair, and the night is young [*Déjà vu*, I thought] our bill is in good hands."

I finished my glass of Silver Oak and yelled, "See you guys." They all held up their glasses, exhaled an odiferous cloud of smoke in my direction and said goodbye.

Rick walked me to the door, shook his head and mumbled, "What a sorry bunch." A month later VECO pulled out of the prison project and the prison bill was carried over onto the following year's agenda.

In December 2005, some people moved in next door to Suite 604. They were quiet folk down from Anchorage for the legislative session. Always the good neighbor, Rick saw a woman opening the door one day and said he hoped his guests weren't too rowdy the night before. Special Agent Kepner turned and assured him the noise and traffic didn't bother her at all, smiled, and bid him a pleasant day.

————·————

"Kepner!"

"Hi Patient, what do you need?" she replied.

"I Just got off the phone with Bill Weimar, you're not going to believe this." I told her about Bill Allen's offer to Ward from the governor's chief of staff. She got pretty excited and told me there was a campaign fundraiser at Allen's house the following Friday. She asked if it would be normal for me to go. I said I went to those things all the time, no problem.

We met the next day in my office. She asked how I was doing. I said I was fine. She smiled and said she'd brought a little something for me to wear to the fundraiser. I was hoping it would be something unobtrusive like a tie tack or lapel flower. Instead, she pulled out a thin little high-tech-looking silver box with a couple of wires attached to it. She pushed something, held the two wires to her mouth, looked at me: "This is agent Kepner, case 04-194a. It's June third, two thousand four and I'm turning this device over to Confidential Source Patient at two-thirty p.m." I began to say something and Kepner held her finger to her lips. "Okay, it's off. Here's how you work this thing..."

The next morning was bright and sunny. *Ah*, I thought, *Chugach Mountains behind, the magnificent Alaska Range across the Inlet, birds singing, a moose grazing in my yard and a wire up my sleeve...life doesn't get any better.* I left my house at about 4:45 p.m. and timed my appearance for the peak of festivities. I parked on the street in front of Senator Ted Stevens' sister's house, fiddled with my device, walked past Federal Judge Sedwick's place and past bumper-to-bumper cars lining both sides of the street. Allen had just moved into the quiet, upscale neighborhood and it occurred to me what a hit he must be with his new neighbors. I sauntered uphill past a "Bootleggers Cove" sign, smiled thinking *there's a fitting name*, and stood panting in front of Allen's two-story makeover. The place was crawling with high-profile politicos, business executives, and a heavy-hitting Republican pastor from the Anchorage Baptist Temple, all crammed elbow to elbow in a large combination great room turned bar, oozing through the kitchen and out the back door.

As I stood in line I said hello to Representatives Lesil McGuire and Tom Anderson and sympathized with them about the paparazzi-style media fixation over their recent domestic violence intervention by Juneau police. Lesil nodded and flapped her doe eyes at Tom as he explained, "It was just a couple beers and a two a.m. post-bowling argument over self-tanning lotion. How can that be *domestic* violence? We're just *close* friends, her husband was up in Anchorage!" I nodded sympathetically, dropped a check in the basket and inked my real name on a tag; I was in!

I moved through the crowd smiling, nodding, and small-talking my way to the bar, where I settled my nerves with a gin and tonic. Drink in hand, I sought my quarry. Kepner had told me there was a female representative who was a person-of-interest I should avoid, because they didn't want to compromise the case they were building about illegal consulting contracts, or something. But just as I spotted Rick Smith, there she was smiling up at me. So, like any well-trained Confidential Source, I sneezed, spilled my drink down her cleavage and apologized as she made her way to the ladies' room.

Drink refreshed, I stalked Smith until he was between encounters. "Hey Rick, how are you?" I asked.

Rick smiled his usual, sodden, two-hours-into-a-fundraiser smile and raised a glass, "Hey pardner, good to see ya." As he bumped and ground his way through the crowd, I discreetly checked for inappropriate wire projections emanating from my body. Rick pulled along my starboard and we talked about the great turnout, various political campaigns, the Tom-and-Lesil affair and other important affairs of state.

Then I leaned in and asked, "Rick, did you guys really offer a job to Jerry Ward if he'd pull out of the senate race?"

Rick laughed and replied, "How in hell you hear that?"

I laughed "I have my sources man. Come on, did you!?"

Rick shrugged "I told Jim Clark and Bill that was a stupid idea. Screw Ward! Talk to Bill if you want the story."

Rick was clearly getting a little cranky and headed to the bar for another drink, so I started looking for Bill Allen. The trail led past some pretty tasty Alaska king crab legs, into the kitchen and out the back door, where I found Bill talking to a couple of lobbyists. He saw me coming, they slipped away, and we shook hands.

"Frank, how's it goin'?" he asked.

"Fine, good turnout, but I'm not much into these things."

He sipped a straight Jack Daniels and gazed out over the inlet. "Me neither. Been out on yer boat?"

"No, not enough time, but I need to change that."

Bill nodded, talked about his Grady sitting up on dry dock for the last two years. "Man, the reds are in the mouth of the Copper River right now and look what we're doin'."

I nodded and asked, "Hey, what's up with Ward? I heard you guys were trying to talk him out of running for the Senate again and he told you to take a hike."

Bill erupted. "That SOB, I offered him a good job, Clark offered him a good job, they're gonna settle his wife's deal. What's wrong with him, anyway? He ain't gonna get a better offer and he's gonna get his ass kicked in the primary, I'll see to that." We agreed that Ward didn't stand much of a chance, but it usually came down to money and Ward seemed to have plenty.

Then someone else caught Bill's attention. As he walked over to say hello, he looked back over his shoulder and asked, "Hey Frank, where do you think he's gettin' all his money?"

I shrugged my shoulders, waved, and walked back down the hill to my car thinking *I know where he's getting his money.*

I drove to a downtown parking garage, circled my way up to the third level and parked in the southeast corner facing a panoramic view of the Chugach Mountains. It was a lovely Alaska evening under a mellow midnight sun. I was watching a group of cantankerous magpies dive-bomb a poor raven lumbering home for the night with a bloated dumpster belly when a car pulled alongside and Kepner hopped in my passenger side. I looked at her and asked, "Could you possibly find more boring cars?"

"They make us less noticeable."

I smiled and thought, *Some understatements are overstated.*

"Well, how'd it go?" Kepner asked. I held my finger to my lips and pointed to the device. She nodded, quietly picked it up and looked at the switch.

"Gotcha," I said. She rolled her eyes, turned the recorder back on, memorialized the mission, turned it off and said, "You are a handful. Come on, how'd it go?"

"The side stripe shrimp on cream-cheese-and-chive crescents were to die for, the fresh Kodiak king crab legs were succulent, the gin was Bombay Sapphire and the conversation was stimulating, and we got our stuff!" I then described the conversations in detail and said, "I knew those guys were probably over the top, but that was incredible."

Kepner said the box would be downloaded and transcribed for the Public Integrity Unit lawyers, then smiled, "Maybe we *should* keep this thing covert for a while longer."

Shortly after the Allen fundraiser the City of Whittier exercised an option to pull out of the private prison contract. Even though a split-the-baby compromise bill authorizing both a private and public prison passed the legislature, the city and everyone else knew the union-controlled Corrections Department would stonewall the project until hell froze over. Of course it helped that Corrections' Deputy Commissioner, Portia Babcock-Parker, was former chief of staff to the split-the-baby compromise prison bill sponsor, Senate Finance co-chair (and soon-to-be senate president) Lyda Green.

Senator Green and her son-in-law, Tuckerman Babcock (a former Alaska Republican Party Chair and brother of Deputy Commissioner Babcock-Parker) both live in the Matanuska-Susitna Valley, and their constituents (well, at least an influential handful of inside traders) had their eyes on the economic stimulus the prison would bring to Valley communities. Being good pro-life conservatives they, of course, had no intention of splitting anybody's baby and eventually succeeded in giving birth to the entire two hundred fifty million dollar construction project in their district. The private prison consortium had been my most time-consuming contract, so after the Allen fundraiser I really didn't have much going on until a most remarkable, serendipitous event.

In Alaska, public corruption cases seem to come in two sizes: dumb and dumber. I was minding my own business, monitoring phone calls and helping Agent Kepner connect dots, when I got a call from a voice out of my past. "Frank, how are you doing?" Though it had been a long time, I immediately recognized the voice of Bill Bobrick, a municipal lobbyist for the same group I was working with, but on a separate project. Bill had heard the private prison was in jeopardy and had an idea.

"Frank, you know I'm working this juvenile treatment program for your friends and it's going pretty good, but I'm not so sure they're gonna renew my contract. You know their top guys better than I do, and they really need me, so I was thinking, if we team up together we could convince them that we can get the prison back on track and seal the deal on the juvenile facility they're after. Now, before you say anything, I think there's a lot of money in this, you know what I mean?" I tried to explain to Bobrick that the prison was DOA, but he pushed on.

"I know, I know, you're missing my point. Do you know Representative Tom Anderson?" he asked. I replied that I did. "Well, Tommy and I are close, *real close*. His, uh, consulting contract with VECO is, uh, about wrapped up. He needs money and I'm trying to pitch a bunch of people to help out. If you could get your guys to hire Anderson, *through me*, he'll be our boy in Juneau."

"What do you mean 'through you'?"

"Well, I'm setting up a little web business called Pacific Publishing, and I'm gonna pay people to write editorial opinions and articles about state and local politics, you know, kind of like the Alaska Digest. Since Tommy will be working for me, he won't have to report the money." I "Uh-huh'ed," and Bobrick went on, "I really think we could do something to get the governor off the pot on the Juvenile approval certificate and the prison. You know Representative Lesil McGuire?" I nodded. "She's Tommy's squeeze and he's promised me that if we take care of him he can deliver Lesil and maybe some others, you know, two votes for the price of one. Why don't we grab lunch and talk about it?" We agreed to meet for lunch at the Southside Bistro in Anchorage at 11:30 a.m. on Wednesday and hung up.

Right after I hung up my phone rang again. This time it was Kepner. "Frank, I have some bad news. I just finished talking to the Public Integrity Unit attorneys. It's a no-go on the Allen fundraiser."

"What do you mean?" I replied. She said they didn't have a prosecutable federal case. I was speechless for a moment, then yelled, "What?! You're gonna tell me a chief of staff to a governor conspires with a high-profile businessman to bribe a former elected official into dropping out of a senate race in exchange for, oh, let me see, about a half million dollars' worth of employment and cash and *it's just fine under federal law?*"

Kepner said, "I know, I know. I talked to my boss and they're sticking to their opinion. But now we know what these guys are capable of." I grunted and changed the subject.

"Hey, I just got off the phone with a voice out of my past and had the weirdest conversation." I went on to describe the Bobrick proposal and asked Kepner what she thought.

She was quiet for a moment and said, "I think you should go to the lunch. Meet me in the parking lot across from my office at ten a.m. tomorrow."

The next morning I pulled into the Office Depot parking lot and waited. In a few minutes Kepner came walking across the lot with a cell phone stuck to her ear laughing about something. She hopped in the passenger side of my old Ford Bronco and said, "Let's go shopping."

"What do you mean?"

"We need to buy you a shirt and JC Penney is right up the street."

I shook my head "JC Penney! I don't buy my clothes at JC Penny." She offered "That's all my budget will handle," so I turned out of the parking lot and headed up the street to Penney's.

"What size?" she asked.

"Oh, a 42, maybe 44."

"All they have is XL and XXL, which do you want?" she asked.

"I'll take the XL. Does it have to be black? I don't wear black."

"Oh, quit being picky. What's wrong with it? I like it," she said as she summoned a clerk, pulled out some cash, "We'll take it." Kepner handed me the bag, I mumbled something about the button-down collar and we walked out of the store.

Back in the car she said, "Drop me off at the corner and give me the shirt. I'll give it back to you before your Wednesday lunch." She jumped out, looked at her watch, gave me a cheesy smile, and walked toward her office. I drove away wondering what I had gotten myself into.

The day before the Bobrick lunch Kepner dropped by my office with the Penny's sack. "Here's your shirt," she said, pulling it out of the bag. "We made a couple of modifications." She smiled, quite full of herself, showed me how everything worked, turned the shirt on and said, "This is Agent Kepner with the FBI, it's ten-thirty a.m. on July…" After she finished recording, she handed the shirt back and said I should just act natural and let Bobrick do the talking. I assured her that was not a problem and she left.

The Southside Bistro is, in my estimation, the best restaurant in Anchorage. It was a bankrupt strip mall pizza joint until a charming and enterprising young chef named Jens turned the place into a mouthwatering, five-star wonder of culinary excellence. The atmosphere, presentation, aroma, flavor, and wine menu transforms the dourest day into a celebration of life. I arrived at the Bistro early to make sure I had a seat that wasn't pointing into the sun and was away from the kitchen and noisier tables.

Bobrick was punctual, as usual, and after ordering and a bit of small talk, got right down to business. "Frank, remember when I said Tommy was two votes for the price of one?" I nodded, leaned in and twisted my torso a bit for better audio and video. "It gets better than that. This guy wants to be a lobbyist and he's so hungry to break into the club he'll do anything for us, I mean a-ny-thingg." Bobrick saw my puzzled look. "Frank, listen to me. If I was a Soviet spy and I was looking for a legislator to recruit, Anderson would be the one, because Anderson needs the monneyy."

At that moment a voice behind us said, "Gentlemen, welcome." It was Jens. Bobrick diverted Jens' attention with an enthusiastic hello while I seized the opportunity to check for protruding wires and nodded with a self-conscious smile. After a bit Jens moved on and Bobrick continued, explaining the structure of the sham company that would accept the payments and launder them back to Anderson.

I nodded, "Uh huh'ed" and actually thought it was quite a clever plan. Had anyone really intended to produce the web site, it might have made legitimate money and given Anderson legitimate income. But why work if you don't have to? I thanked Bobrick for lunch and told him I could come up with some money, but needed to be sure of Anderson.

Bobrick enthusiastically replied, "Tell you what, I'll have him give you a call." I said that would be great, we shook hands, waved to Jens, and left the restaurant.

I drove out the parking lot, spotted Kepner blending in with her surroundings, picked up my cell, dialed, and waved as I drove by. "Kepner, that's a real nice beige Taurus you're sitting in. See you at my office." At the office Kepner said she heard the whole conversation.

We talked a little more strategy and she said, "Well, let me know if

Tommy calls." I handed her the Penney's bag and she headed downtown to download the shirt. I knew she was dying to see the pictures.

The call from Anderson came a few days later. Bubbling with enthusiasm, "Tommy" (as Bobrick called him) assured me that he'd carry our water on the juvenile Certificate of Need, the prison, and anything else we needed. We agreed on twenty four thousand dollars in three payments between August and December. He said the checks needed to be made out to Pacific Publishing and Bobrick would "take care" of him out of another account. Anderson said that way, "No one can ever…if anyone ever says I should have reported the money I say, *Hey, I work for Bobrick, I don't know what the hell you're talking about.*" I told Anderson the Department of Corrections was dragging its feet on the private prison feasibility study required by the enabling legislation, and I needed his help. Anderson offered, "I'll just call the commissioner and say you better get the study done!" I thanked him and we hung up.

Representative Anderson was very enthusiastic and turned out to be a real bargain. Over the next few months he wrote letters, made phone calls, attended meetings and sent e-mails attempting to resolve a variety of benign or fictitious issues facing his benefactors. Shortly before the 2005 legislative session he even called to reassure me he would be covering my bases during the session, including casting votes on my behalf. "Ya know, when you kinda giggle and say, *hey Tom, we're doing this to help you, it's really not for your web thing,* I mean, unless you want me to quit the legislature and, you know, work for you. But no, you don't want that. You want votes in the legislature."

I said, "Tom, relax, don't worry, you're earning your money. By the way, I've got another check for eight grand."

Tommy replied, "Awesome, awesome. I appreciate it."

Kepner leaned over the laptop, listened to Anderson, shook her head and thought *Frank was right, this thing's going to get big, real big. Wait 'til he hears what…*a phone interrupted and Kepner picked up. "Yeah, uh-huh, we got the federal magistrate's permission? Killer! Let's set up." She looked across the table. "Chad, tell the techies to get right up here. I'll call headquarters; we're gonna need help."

Chapter Three
Multi-tasking

The year 2004 was shaping up to be very productive. We had enough to seal the lid on Anderson and Bobrick. There were good leads on Bill Allen, Rick Smith, and the Suite 604 regulars. State Representative Vic Kohring was in the crosshairs and some feelers were looking very fruitful on U.S. Senator Ted Stevens, president of the senate Pro Tempore (*and* third in succession to the President of the United States), Alaska senator Ben Stevens (the elder Stevens' son) and U.S. Congressman Don Young. Then there was former Alaska state senator Jerry Ward.

Sadly, former senator Ward suffers from Chronic PMS (Politico Maniosis Syndrome), a condition that manifests itself by obsessive-compulsive cravings to eat, sleep, and drink politics whether in office or out, twenty-four hours a day, seven days a week. He's a charming and versatile fellow who dances between and around political parties, ethical restraints, and legal boundaries like a Heisman Trophy running back. After warming the political bench for years, Ward's defining moment occurred during the 1990 Alaska gubernatorial race.

John Lindauer, a wealthy Alaskan news mogul, was running for governor on the Alaska Independent Party ticket and Ward was his lieutenant Governor. Alaska senator Arliss Sturgulewski won the Republican Primary, but she was a bit too liberal for the more conservative Alaskan Republicans who wear real fur and support a woman's right to *bare* arms and babies. So a month before the election, Lindauer and Ward (whom nobody really took seriously) and the AIP Chairman (a guy named Vogler) had an epiphany: They knew the AIP ticket was a long shot because a majority of Alaska voters were right-of-center, but not as far right as the AIP. The polls clearly showed that left-of-center Sturgulewski was stuck in a neck-and-neck race with her Democrat opponent, Tony Knowles. So, a month before the election, they cut a deal with ever popular former governor and U.S. Interior Secretary Wally Hickel, held a press conference, and in a show of conservative solidarity, announced that Lindauer and Ward were stepping aside to support Hickel and Coghill on the AIP ticket. Well, the rest is history. Wally and Jack swept the election and moved to the capital.

Lindauer became an interesting footnote in Alaska politics, nothing to do with this story. Let's just say he won't be returning any time soon. Wiley Ward, on the other hand, cut a sweet deal with Hickel and Coghill. He was appointed a special assistant to the governor and his wife was appointed director of the governor's office in Anchorage. Ward, an Alaska Native, was a bit of a free spirit who moved about Hickel's four-year term as a "special assistant," laying the ground work for his own political futures by introducing sweat-lodge ceremonies to high-security prisons, castigating various governor's aides as *queers* and *gigolos*, coaching his wife in the fine art of sex discrimination entrapment, and tending to House Speaker Ramona Barnes' need for inside information about the governor.

It was Barnes who introduced and added Ward to a select group of personal concierges and advisors that included VECO *Suite 604* Bill Allen and *Less Costly* Bill Weimar. As a powerful, single, middle-aged woman of immense stature and personality, Barnes relied on Allen's and Weimar's altruistic emotional and financial support for such incidentals as property maintenance, campaign donations, and policy advice on complex prison and oil industry issues facing the state. As an apprentice concierge, Ward mostly tended Barnes' dry cleaning, neurotic schnauzer, and messenger services. But the apprenticeship paid off. In 1996, two years after Hickel retired as governor, Ward won his race for the Alaska Senate, with a little help from Ramona's friends.

Ward was now back in his element plotting and scheming his way around the capital for six unremarkable years until losing *his* seat after Democrats reapportioned *his* district. Outed and simmering, Ward sat on the sidelines selling real estate until the 2004 election, when he rallied forces to retake his rightful senate seat. Unfortunately, Ward's biggest defender and apologist, Ramona Barnes, had died the year before. During the interim, Ward got seriously cross-threaded with VECO Bill Allen who, as we learned at the fundraiser, was intent on keeping Ward out of the 2004 election. Broke, with a six-figure campaign facing him, Ward called on the only person he knew who had the incentive, energy, creativity, and finances to help him win: Bill Weimar.

"Okay, okay," Kepner replied. "Right now all I need is someone in Montana where Weimar lives and someone in Seattle to trace any transactions. Chad, Joleen, and I can handle Alaska. But I tell ya, this thing is spreading like a virus. We need to stay on top of things as they unfold." Kepner paused and braced for the response.

"Do you think I'm stupid!? yelled Kepner's SAC (Special Agent in Charge). "I know you've been talking to headquarters. They think you're eff'n Shirley Sherlock Holmes incarnate! Well, you wanna know what I think? I think you want me to look bad! Homeland Security is our priority; you know, *Ben Laydun*, suicide bombers, terrorists. And what have you been doing...?" Kepner's cell phone rang. They stared at each other until the SAC said, "Well, answer it! And maybe you can keep me *just a little* in the loop when you're not sucking up to head-quarters; shut my door on the way out!"

Kepner eased out, looked at her caller ID, took a deep breath, and whispered, "Yeah Chad, what's up?"

Chad replied, "What's up is I think we found the source of Ward's campaign funding. Weimar's been buying or financing a round robin of real estate exchanges between Ward, himself, and Ward's friends and relatives that look phony as a three-dollar bill. But Ward's panicked he's gonna lose the election and we think Weimar's going to transfer a bundle of cash through a Seattle contact to help him out."

Kepner thought for a moment and said, "Listen Chad, I think Weimar's played fast and loose with a bankruptcy, an off-shore trust, campaign contributions, bogus corporations, money laundering, and creative accounting, but most of his stuff is beyond federal statutes of limitation. Unless we can add it all up to RICO racketeering, and the Public Integrity attorneys don't think we can, we need something solid and current. See if you can find out what Ward promised in return for the money. If he wins the elections, wire fraud and bribery convictions will give 'em both plenty of time to think about how lucky they are we weren't on to them ten years ago."

Kepner hung up. Smiling she mumbled, "Hmm, 'Shirley Sherlock Holmes?' Why, thank you my dear Watson."

———•———

Bill Weimar is bigger than life. Six-feet-six, three hundred pounds, and sporting a monstrous Afro, Weimar headed up the Alcan and crossed into Alaska during the late '60s, driving a Volkswagon hippie van belching pungent clouds of exhaust, marijuana and Credence Clearwater Revival. Inside a payload of *Students for a Democratic Society* were planning a model utopian community in the Last Frontier. By the late '70s the group of *Young Democrats* had congealed into an energetic, free-spirited, pipe-tokin', pill stokin', anything snortin', sexually liberated political force that overthrew the Alaska Democratic Party, seized control of the legislature and penetrated, so to speak, the highest levels of government. Most attribute the *Young Democrat Ad Hoc* political success to the strategic and diabolically brilliant mind of Bill Weimar.

Unfortunately, Weimar was a lightning rod of controversy, and after two unsuccessful bids for office (and a penchant for generating brown paper bags brimming with cash campaign "contributions"), found he was an untouchable on the outskirts of the new order he helped create. Lobbyist friend and mentor Lew Dischner fed and clothed him during those days, and after Dischner was convicted of racketeering, Weimar supported his family until Lew got out of prison. Weimar credits himself a "stand-up guy" who takes care of his friends. His disappointment that the *Young Democrats* (who owed their very positions and future to Weimar's political savvy) weren't "stand-up guys" was a bitter pill that Weimar never got over.

After Weimar figured out that no one was gonna take care of Weimar but Weimar, he traded his socialist ideology for a more pragmatic version of progressive capitalism: selling the state what the state was already doing, at lower cost. His formula was simple, but deadly: anticipate a growing need; establish an answer to the need; change the law to allow the private sector to meet the need; and, after winning the contract, amend the law to restrict competition to fill the need. It worked like a charm with the growing prison population. By the late '80s Weimar controlled the lion's share of Alaska's multimillion dollar halfway house contracts and had influenced enough enactments, revisions, and amendments to state and local legislation to accommodate his ever increasing flow of clients.

The key to Weimar's strategy was political influence. He relied on public policymakers and managers in key positions to make the changes that would protect and grow his business. The changes were always "necessary" to provide "better service at lower cost to the state." There was really nothing wrong, and a lot right, about Weimar's pitch, so political support wasn't difficult to muster, particularly among his new Republican friends. The devil wasn't in what, it was in how he employed his influence. Weimar understood that public policy and policymakers ebb and flow to the benefit and detriment of special interests. His special interest was making money from government contracts and that required special friends who supported his various enterprises. And the key to special friends in politics is money, and right about now a lot of Weimar's former special friends are breathing deep sighs of relief as they read my generic passing reference to their *special* relationship with the big guy.

As a budding young entrepreneur, Weimar learned that political radioactivity diminishes in direct proportion to campaign contribution generosity and net worth. Weimar never really abandoned his liberal roots or loyalty to the Democratic Party, most of his old political cronies abandoned him. So when Weimar demonstrated the commitment and financial wherewithal to generate astonishing amounts of financial support for his old Ad Hoc friends (or anyone else who was willing to advance his interests), all was forgiven.

It's hard to find a middle-aged Alaska politician of any stature who didn't ask for and receive generous support (in one form or another) from Weimar. But some were particularly close and willing to go to remarkable sword-falling lengths on Ol' Bill's behalf. And one of those was former Alaska Senator Jerry Ward.

———

Kepner needed to learn the layout of Ward's house and where he kept his records. She knew he had a cabin on a lake somewhere near Caswell and an old mobile home on the Kenai Peninsula, but she thought he was physically operating out of his daughter's house in south Anchorage because at least half of his phone calls came from that number. She remembered Ward's daughter was a realtor and Patient had bought one of her listings a year or two before and thought *I wonder whether he could drop by for a peek without appearing too obvious.*

"Patient? This is Kepner. I need a favor."

"Oh boy, what now?"

"You think you can swing by Ward's daughter's house and see if you think Ward lives there too?"

I answered, "Yeah, sure, when?"

"Anytime soon," she replied.

"*Any time soon?*" I echoed.

"Did they teach you to speak oxymoron at the academy? When do you want me to go, *anytime*, or *soon?*"

"Smart ass! Whenever you can" she replied.

"Okay, I'll call you when I'm done." After we hung up I thought *what the heck, I'm not doing anything special. I think I'll take a drive.*

I looked up the address and was surprised to learn Ward's daughter lived only a mile or two away. No wonder Ward wanted to plant one of his campaign signs in my front yard. I drove up Rabbit Creek Road, took a right onto Bridgeview Drive and wandered around a bit before I found the address. I parked in front and walked up to the door. It was a very attractive cream with blue trim; a custom tri-level in an upscale neighborhood, with desirable southern exposure and a great view of the Inlet. I knocked but no one answered. I rang the bell and no one answered. I turned to leave, heard the door swing open, turned back around and there stood Ward's thirty-something daughter, bare-assed naked, dripping wet and wrapped in a towel that from north to south exposed, well, the better part of her geography.

"Frank!" she exclaimed.

Looking her in the eyes, I said, "Uhh, hi. Is the senator home?"

"No, come on in. How arrre you?" she asked.

"Well I, uh, I can come back later. Just tell him I dropped by," I stammered.

"No, no, come on in. It's great to see you again," she said with alarming enthusiasm. "The baby's down for a nap."

Between wondering what she meant and how I was going to explain this to my wife, I stepped inside and said, "Well, okay, just for a minute, gee, nice place."

Smiling, she flipped her hair, said, "Yeah, let me show you around," turned and gave me a widescreen tour of nooks, crannies, and crevices that also included her new house and Ward's downstairs apartment. At the door we said goodbye and I walked to my old Bronco smiling over how proud she was of her new house.

I called Kepner, thanked her for the assignment and gave a graphic description of the exterior, interior, view and layout, including the location of the stuff Kepner was really interested in. "Good job" Kepner said laughing.

"All in the cause of justice, Sherlock," I replied and hung up.

———•———

Ward lost his 2004 race for the senate. Since he had no campaign contributions to report, it seems an interested press (and, evidently, voters) just didn't buy that he funded his six-digit campaign out of his own pocket. Neither did Kepner. But there was another interesting turn of events that had her attention. In a post election poll, the Alaska House Majority Caucus voted to dump Pete Kott as House Speaker in favor of Representative John Harris. A week later Kott organized (with a little nudge from his VECO friends) a dozen breakaway Republicans (including Tom Anderson and Lesil McGuire), formed a coalition with thirteen Democrats and staged a coup to seize control of the House. The insurrection was quashed when Republican Party heavies weighed in and threatened the rebels. Some were reprimanded, some stripped of chairmanships and others relegated to benign committees. All, that is, except Lesil McGuire, who retained her Judiciary Chair through a display of teary, doe-eyed contrition that would melt any heart. Stripped of any apparent position of influence, Kott became a free agent.

By Christmas 2004 Kepner thought she had enough to indict Weimar, Bobrick, Anderson, and possibly Ward (one of the Public Integrity lawyers had a technical problem with Ward's case that he was still trying to work out). But Kott and several other big fish seemed to be schooling in and around the waters of Suite 604 and she didn't want to scare them off with the publicity the charges would generate. Besides, at the right time they just might prove useful. For the next few months she just needed to be patient, develop her cases, observe the legislative session and do background checks on the revolving door of legislators, lobbyists, hookers, and others who frequented Suite 604 on a regular basis. And the first name on her list was Alaska Senate Rules chair John Cowdery.

Cowdery is a seventy-something legislative retread who had a successful pipeline boom construction company. He served with Ramona Barnes for a term in 1982, got bounced and then reappeared well after he should have retired with some remaining semblance of dignity. Before her death, a concerned Representative Barnes carried Cowdery's water, trying to convince whoever would listen that 'ol John was still at the top of his game. In many respects, he was.

Over the years of power and privilege Cowdery developed a robust appetite for culinary and other pleasures of the flesh and built a solid reputation for willingness to swap votes and inside information for cravings satiation. John was also a seasoned mariner who, during the corruption investigations, purchased and transported Heeere's Johnny! Ed McMann's 60 foot motor yacht up the west coast to Alaska. A vessel with the style and sea handling of a '70s Winnebago which, under Cowdery's command, narrowly averted disaster a half dozen times over a three month journey that ordinarily takes about six weeks. I happened to be at his homeport of Whittier the day he pulled into the marina.

Cowdery's wife's name is Juanita. John purchased and christened the new seagoing motor home *Johnita II* a short time before the smaller *Johnita I* caught fire and sank while Cowdery coincidentally stepped aboard the only passing vessel within thirty miles. As *Johnita II* approached the harbor, fear that Cowdery would actually try to dock the lumbering party barge swept through the marina like wildfire. Boat owners ran from every direction screaming instructions, throwing dock lines, laying out protective bumpers, then collapsing with relief as *Johnita II* swept past their vessels, crunched into a loading dock and unleashed a tidal surge reminiscent of the Great Alaska Earthquake tsunami of '64.

John disembarked alone complaining that his crew had abandoned ship somewhere off the west coast of Oregon after the anchor took leave of its senses, dispatched itself in a suicidal plunge to the sea floor and refused to come back aboard. Evidently John's crew thought the anchor dive was some kind of seafaring omen and hailed a ride to shore with a passing coast guard cutter.

One week later Cowdery took a boatload of wedding guests to the College Fjord glaciers and grounded the vessel on a shallow moraine. He hosted the wedding and reception listing thirty five degrees to starboard and cruised home on the next tide, after a little tug from a friend. Waving, shouting, hoisting champagne bottles and toasting the marina in relief, wedding guests stared as boat owners throughout the marina dropped what they were doing, abandoned slips and ran screaming instructions, throwing dock lines, laying out protective bumpers and collapsing with relief as *Johnita* surged past sporting a tasteful twelve foot streamer of seaweed, kelp, mussels, and glacier silt from her bowsprit, fashioned, no doubt, for the occasion.

About a month later I got a call from a friend at the harbor. "Frank?" said the voice.

"Don, what's up?" I answered.

"You know Cowdery's new boat?" he asked.

"Yeah, what a tub," I replied.

"Remember the pilothouse door about twelve feet above the water?" he asked again.

"Yeah?" I replied.

"Well, you can walk into 'er level with the dock. She sank in the harbor last night."

I didn't think much again about *Johnita II* until I received a call during the 2005 legislative session. "Patient, this is Kepner."

Ahh I thought, *a voice out of my past.* "Hi Kepner, nice to hear from you. Where ya been?"

"Oh, the usual, hey, you have a boat in Whittier. Did you ever hear anything about John Cowdery's boat *Johnita II* sinking?" she asked.

"Sure, but it's a long story," I replied.

"Well, I think it's sitting in VECO Bill Allen's yard at the Port of Anchorage being repaired and upgraded. Would you be able to identify it?" she asked.

I laughed, "Well, it's a pretty unassuming little vessel, but I think so,"

Kepner pleaded, "Come on, can you do it right away?"

"You bet, anything for the cause. Will it be as much fun as finding Ward's apartment?"

Kepner crinkled her nose and replied, "Thanks, now I'll have nightmares of ol' jelly-belly Cowdery dripping wet in a skimpy bath towel. Get to work and let me know what you find."

Kepner hung up, turned to her computer, typed *www.veco.com* and smiled wryly as she scrolled through the company's core values: *Good Corporate Citizen - VECO and its employees participate in and contribute to community activities.* "You're telling me. A major yacht upgrade and millions of dollars in backroom political polls, consultants and campaign *contributions* since 1990, and who knows what else," she mumbled.

The website boasted annual revenues of six hundred sixty five million dollars. The corporation employed more than four thousand people and had offices in the United States, Canada, the United Arab Emirates, and India. From other sources Kepner learned that VECO CEO Bill Allen was an oil field welder and roughneck who moved to Alaska in the early '70s to work on Cook Inlet oil platforms. He started a fledgling oil service company a few years later, cozied up to the producers' anti-union predisposition and grew the company, until a disastrous 1982 investment in a Houston shipyard ended in bankruptcy. With Arco's and SOHIO's support, VECO reorganized and added a new service line: political activism. And although there's no evidence that the producers were behind it, oil field folklore has it that Allen sold his birthright to carry the oil giants' political water in exchange for sole-source oil field contracts.

The new service line was, in fact, delivered with such enthusiasm that in 1985 VECO was fined by the Alaska Public Offices Commission for a scheme that funneled secret donations to candidates through employee deductions. VECO's oil industry public service award came in 1989 when Exxon sole-sourced VECO as the oil spill cleanup contractor to mop up Prince William Sound after an Exxon Valdez oil tanker ran aground on Bligh Reef, dumping millions of gallons of oil into north gulf coast waters.

Allen used the oil spill profits to purchase the *Anchorage Times*, one of Alaska's two largest newspapers and conservative alternative to the more progressive *Anchorage Daily News*. Only three years later, after a vicious subscriber war with the *Daily News*, Allen conceded there wasn't enough room in Anchorage for the two papers and closed the *Times*, but not before cutting a deal that secured an editorial half page opposite the *Daily News* editorial page. The *Voice of the Times* became the voice for the oil industry and, some would say, political podium for Bill Allen. Whatever the motivation, the *VECO Times* (as it was bitingly referred to by anyone left of center) shaped public thought and policy as VECO expanded into the global oil economy.

From discreet interviews, Kepner learned that Bill Allen was the stuff legends were made of. As a younger man he had a rough-and-tumble preference for whiskey, fast horses and loose women. In maturity his taste shifted to politics, Silver Oak and ladies of substance, in that order. Political influence was Allen's strategic pathway to money, sex and power. He was selected Alaskan of the Year in 1994 and had direct access to the highest offices in state and federal government, including his good friends U.S. Senator Ted Stevens and U.S. Congressman Don Young, two of the most senior and powerful men in Congress. But even in his aggressive, insatiable drive to deliver results for big oil, Allen was disarmingly simple in dress and manner, a tall, lumbering, good ol' boy who could put his arm around you and talk about fishin' while he was peein' on your Tony Lamas. Kepner turned off her computer and called it a day.

———•———

At the start of the 2005 Alaska legislative session the state of the state was looking pretty sweet. After a dozen years of fiscal doom and gloom, lawmakers found themselves mud wrestling over how to spend a six hundred fifty three million dollar windfall created by surging oil prices. Dividing the pork was a delightful diversion from the hand-wringing of previous years, but the legislature was also acutely aware that the real game was on the third floor of the capitol building where the governor's people were negotiating terms for a gas pipeline with the big boys: BP, Exxon Mobile, and ConocoPhillips.

The incentive to build another Alaska pipeline comes from thirty five trillion cubic feet of "stranded" gas the producers have been sitting on for the past thirty years, as well as an estimated two hundred fifty trillion cubic feet which lie beneath the surface of Alaska's National Petroleum Reserve. A gas line from the North Slope, through Canada, to the Midwestern United States, would move 4.5 billion cubic feet of gas, *per day*, at a projected annual market value of nearly 6 billion dollars. In 2005, the estimated cost to bring the gas to market through a new pipeline was twenty billion dollars. It's understandable, then, that simply wrapping the Legislatures' collective mind around the magnitude of the event would consume more gas-fired hot air than a normal session, as well as keep VECO and oil industry lobbyists very busy grooming the desired result.

Despite Third Floor (governor's office) assurance to the contrary, by the end of the 2005 session there was no gas line contract for the legislature to review, let alone ratify. But excitement over the prospect of a special-session gas line agreement was palpable at *Sine Die*, at least until the next day, when New Jersey pollster *SurveyUSA* announced that former U.S. Senator and current Alaska Governor Frank Murkowski had earned the second-lowest approval rating of any governor in U.S. history, second only to Ohio Governor Robert Taft who, at the time, was facing criminal charges for failing to report a few gifts.

Murkowski was elected governor of Alaska on November 5, 2002, by overwhelming mandate. His popularity headed downhill immediately after he appointed his daughter, Lisa Murkowski, to fill his seat in the United States Senate. No one really questioned Murkowski's hanging on to the senate seat while running for governor because most Alaskans understood the value of congressional seniority: If he lost the race for governor, he would simply go back to his Energy Chair and continue shoveling pork and favors to Alaska. Not that he was that good at it.

Other than twenty unremarkable years riding U.S. Senator Ted Stevens' coattails, about the most memorable pork Murkowski delivered was stopping the U.S. Forest Service from closing the outhouses at Turnagain Pass, a scenic road that leads from Anchorage to the Kenai Peninsula. In a press release saying, "I'm not going to take this sitting down," Murkowski urged the Forest Service to "flush out their pending business and push hard to find a solution." After the Forest Service agreed to leave the restrooms open, a relieved Murkowski said, "I'm delighted that the agency was able to wipe away any public discomfort." In spite of his less than remarkable congressional record, no one dreamed *Governor* Murkowski's first executive act would be to bypass customary process and appoint his own daughter to a seat in the United States Senate, particularly when, only four months earlier, she had narrowly defeated a *fellow Republican* challenge to her own unremarkable two terms in the Alaska House by a mere fifty seven votes.

Blatant nepotism, ethically challenged appointees, a private jet purchased with overwhelming public and legislative disapproval, slicing aid to elderly Alaskans, and introducing a bill to strip pension and medical benefits from state employees eventually took a toll on the governor's popularity. While some just chalk it up to breathtaking, mule-headed arrogance, by 2005 ol' Murky just didn't sit well with seventy three percent of the population. So, to most Alaskans, the prospect of Frank Murkowski negotiating an acceptable, untainted deal with the oil companies was a fantasy. But as Murkowski's popularity plummeted, VECO Bill Allen kept reminding his executive staff, "So long as ol' Murky gits us ar deal, ta hy'ell what people think of 'im."

In spite of the gas line, the 2005 legislative session wasn't a total bust for the government. I was given the opportunity to wine and dine Representatives Kohring, Anderson, and McGuire and gleaned some insight, as well as some extraordinary sound and footage (by that time I was pretty good at espio-tech) implicating Kohring and exculpating McGuire. For Representative McGuire, the issue was whether she knew Tommy (Representative Anderson) was selling *her* votes to the highest bidder. So, in mid-February, we dined together in the Gold Room of the Baronof Hotel. Three hours, one visibly nervous Anderson and three bottles of wine later (while McGuire engaged a passing admirer in a sidebar conversation) Tommy leaned in my direction and whispered, "Frank, uh, she doesn't know about our deal, so, you know what I mean?" I interrupted, put my hand on Tom's arm, leaned in for a close-up and assured him I understood.

Much later that night a sleepy Kepner picked up. "Geez, Patient, how am I supposed to explain filet mignon, flaming *fresh* spotted shrimp, stuffed *fresh* Prince William Sound oysters, three bottles of vintner's choice, dessert, and cognac chasers! I told her truth and justice come at a high price and to stop whining, her SAC would understand. Besides, we now had evidence that Lesil McGuire wasn't corrupt, she just had a weakness for low-hanging fruit.

The Kohring dinner wasn't all that eventful either. But after two hours of appetizers, house specials, dessert, another round of appetizers and a take-home doggy bag, I was able to establish Kohring's "red-carpet" list of oil industry supporters, his propensity to cater to the oil producers' beck and call, and his unbelievable (I'm talking Guinness Records potential) capacity to consume massive quantities of anything that's put in front of him. He also mentioned that Eric Musser (a former legislative aide) really got him in trouble with VECO Bill Allen by filing an ethics complaint against former representative and FBI person-of-interest Beverly Masek, one of Allen's shill legislators. After taking emergency leave to help his ailing mother, Musser returned to find his job filled by someone new, a tidbit that engendered a bit of jury ill will at Kohring's later trial for bribery, conspiracy, and extortion.

After the 2005 session Kepner paid a little visit to lobbyist Bill Bobrick and his buddy, Representative "Tommy" Anderson. There were strong indications that they both could be helpful clarifying the roles and activities of several persons of interest to the FBI. Bobrick was extremely cooperative in exchange for certain accommodations that were promised to kick in after he produced the fruit of the agreement. Anderson was equally cooperative and, by midsummer, put the government over the top on the legal basis required to wiretap VECO Smith's and Allen's personal cells and phone lines.

The incredible thing is only a week or two after Kepner and her people squeezed the last drop of useful information out of his hide, Anderson rescinded his cooperation agreement. Evidently, Representative McGuire, Tom's newly divorced, newly with-child wife-to-be, thought he should have cut a sweeter deal for his efforts. You see, Tom knew he was in a lot of trouble and with his people pleasing nature cooperating with the FBI came real easy. But he also knew he would eventually have to tell Representative McGuire about the seriousness of his little problem, he just needed, "the right time and place."

So shortly before the legislature's 2005 spring recess, Tom told Kepner he planned to tell Lesil about the whole affair in Hawaii during the recess. Kepner didn't hear from Tom for several weeks, but it soon became apparent that, instead of explaining his criminal affair, Tom had put all of his energy into sealing the deal on his romantic affair with Lesil, or so it seemed from the joyous press release announcing the two lovebirds were getting married *and* having a baby.

Kepner had a fit when she read the announcement and told Tom that if he didn't tell his wife-to-be about his little problem, she'd do it for him. A chastened and whiny Tom expressed concern over Lesil's fragile state, but agreed he would tell her. Now, there's no record of when or where Tommy finally bared his soul, or of his future wife's reaction, because the government can't wiretap people just for marrying dumb. But a fall government meeting with Tom and Lesil led many to believe Tom may have slightly underestimated the gravity of his condition, because after listening quietly to the U.S. Attorneys explain the charges against Tom, Lesil declined an offer to review the wire evidence, took Tom's hand, fired his attorney and told Kepner to take a hike, in a pouty, faux-outraged sort of way.

Now it's important to understand that both Lesil and Tom have law degrees from very prestigious universities, but having failed the bar, neither is licensed to practice law. So, as they say in court, both Tom and Lesil were *well advised in the premises*. Kepner, who was *well advised in the consequences*, shrugged her shoulders and wondered whether they could sue each other for malpractice.

———————

For Kepner and her small team, the summer of 2005 felt a lot like herding chickens. I was busy monitoring calls, offering analysis on back-alley political moves and helping to establish a basis for wiretapping Suite 604. Chad was up to his neck in father/son senators Ben and Ted Stevens' offshore fisheries maneuvers, a TDY agent on loan from Texas was tracking leads on the growing list of *persons of interest*, and Kepner was sandwiched between enlisting more help from headquarters and managing the growing caseload. She was also keeping a close eye on former House Speaker and now free-range representative Pete Kott, who managed Kott's Hardwood Flooring in Eagle River, Alaska.

By *manage* I mean that during the legislative interim ol' Pete managed to get down on his hands and knees, prepare the subsurface, and lay hardwood floors alongside his son, who ran the business during the session. Toward the end of a particularly unremarkable construction season, Pete groaned, stood up, looked at his swollen knees and bruised fingers, and decided he'd had enough. He picked up his phone and, courtesy of Kott's friend and associate Tom Anderson, dialed VECO vice president Rick Smith's heavily monitored phone line. "Rick?" he asked.

"Hi Pete, what's up?" Smith replied.

"I need a job."

"You've got a job. Get us a pipeline," Rick replied.

"I just want to be the warden in Barbados [where VECO was general contractor in a prison construction project]."

"And I just want a gas pipeline," Smith replied and hung up.

Smith's tough-love approach was evidently enough. On January 8, 2006, the day before the new legislative session, Kott called Bill Allen and left him a message: "Bill, Pete. Things start tomorrow. I just wanted to get what our instructions are." The next day Kott assured Allen, "I'm going to get this gas line done so I can get out of here."

Allen urged, "Get the gas. Get the gas."

"That's my commitment to you, so I'll get 'er done."

Allen replied, "And I'll do the same for you."

Allen turned to Smith and complained that their lobbyist was wasting too much time with Kott and needed to work the other legislators, because "we got more money in Pete Kott than he can even think about."

Chapter Four
The Corrupt Bastards Club

"Ahh, what a sweet world we live in. Satellites that can read license plates, thermal imaging that scan through walls, video the size of a pin, and audio that can pick up a cricket passing gas at a hundred yards, these are the best of times," Kepner mumbled as she adjusted a headset and positioned herself in front of the monitor, half a ham sandwich, Hershey's Kisses, and bottled water close at hand. Within minutes, a rattling sound and slow squeak announced a medium-built white male and attractive blonde as they entered the room and came into view. Kepner leaned into the screen and watched them cross the room. The man cracked his knuckles, sat on the couch, and watched as the woman walked to the bedroom door. She turned, lifted a cell phone to her ear and whispered, "Kepner, can you see us? How's the audio? I don't know, that kitchen area's gonna be tough to cover." It had been a long day, but when every square inch of Suite 604 was finally covered, Kepner smiled, thinking of things to come.

———

With only fifty years since statehood, it's hard to say whether former Alaska governor and U.S. Senator Frank Murkowski will remain the second-least-popular Governor in U.S. history, but to his credit, he was the only one able to jump-start negotiations with the major oil producers over building a natural gas pipeline. With declining oil production and diminishing revenue, the talks were of immense importance to the state and VECO, whose bread was buttered by BP, Exxon, and ConocoPhillips, the major oil producers. Finally, on February 21, 2006…, after more than a year of closed-door negotiations, Murkowski announced the State had reached an agreement on construction of a pipeline, contingent, of course, on significant changes in the way the state taxed oil production. The contingencies were simple enough to understand: if the Legislature didn't approve the proposed changes, the agreement was dead.

Murkowski immediately introduced a new Petroleum Profits Tax (PPT) system and urged fast-track approval by the legislature. The new system was based on a percentage of the producer's net profits, meaning a simple formula of revenues minus capital and operating expenditures. From the net, the producers would pay taxes at a twenty percent rate and receive a twenty percent tax credit. The *20/20* formula was the hottest topic in the 2006 legislative session and getting that bill passed was Ted Stevens', Frank Murkowski's and Bill Allen's number one priority. To many, the *20/20 on net* was based on the gross reality that the former were caught in the major oil producers' net, but not Wasilla Representative Vic Kohring.

Wasilla, Alaska is a spectacular one-hour drive north of Anchorage. The city was founded in 1917 as a convenient place to stop the train and allow exuberant trappers and miners to off-load and seek their fortunes. It was named after the Dena'ina Indian chief Wasilla, whose name meant "breath of air," though some traditions say the chief's name spelled backwards (*All I Saw*) was the real namesake. Today, the Wasilla city limits meander around hundreds of small lakes and through a forest of white birch which contain the habitat for a disproportionately high number of right-wing voters who mate in and around the area. In Alaska House District 14, "if yer politics are somewhere between Birch (not to be confused with the tree) and Limbaugh, why straight talkin', sheet rockin', commie knockin', government sockin' Vic Kohring is yer man."

Vic was elected to the State House in 1994 and enjoyed remarkable reelection margins, despite claiming residence at his parents' Wasilla mobile home while living in Portland, Oregon with his Russian e-bride and her daughter. As Wasilla's "Alaska tuxedo hardworking ultraconservative," Kohring walked his talk by conserving resources as well as traditional values. During the legislative session, Kohring conserved housing by sleeping on his office couch. He conserved water by using the capitol building public bathrooms for personal hygiene. He conserved food and fossil fuel by walking to nearby hotels to graze on special-interest receptions and buffets. But mostly, he conserved votes by reserving a good portion of *his* to leverage the special interests of those willing to subsidize his conservative lifestyle.

Staying in touch with constituents was among Kohring's core values, so two weeks into the 2006 legislative session, Kohring thought he should check in with VECO and offer support on the PPT. He dialed the Baranof Hotel and asked to be connected to Suite 604. After a couple of rings Rick Smith picked up. "Hi, Rick here."

Kohring replied, "Rick, just called to let you and Mr. Allen know I'm willing to help if there's any issues that come up this session."

Smith looked across the room at Allen, pointed to the phone and held his nose. "Thanks Vic, we're really monitoring the PPT bill and gas line legislation. Our future's riding on this and the legislature could kill the goose, if you know what I mean."

"Right, any points you want me to make in caucus, committee meetings, on the radio, any questions that need to be asked, any information you need, just let me know," Vic said.

"Good, we'll be in touch. Drop by sometime." Smith hung up. Bill Allen looked up from his paper and said, "I just gave him a thousand in cash and promised his nephew a job. He'll kiss our, *now what?* Go ahead, answer it."

"Pete, my man, how are ya?" Smith fumbled with his cell, put it up to his good ear and said, "How's it going in DC?"

Kott whispered, "Jusht checkin' in, havin' dinner with 'em right now. You know where my allegiansh is, so ya know, just, you're my besht buddy, you can count on it, that's why I call you up on this crap, right? So's you can fill me in on some of this shit I'm not aware of."

Smith rolled his eyes at Allen as he hung up the phone and said, "Kott's drunk. By the way, we made the arrangements for his cousin, or whatever's school board race. You heard anything from Weyhrauch?"

"Yeah, he wants to talk to me about the oil tax and other stuff," replied Allen.

———— • ————

Back from DC, Pete Kott knocked on the door of Suite 604. Smith opened, glanced down the hallway and said, "Pete, what's goin' on?"

Kott groaned, "Pour me a tall one. What a day! Ten weeks into the session and those guys are all over the board on the PPT! I had to give up some chits to stuff Dyson's anti-abortion bill where the sun don't shine and I've got him over a barrel. If he wants his bill he'd better square up on oil taxes, 'cause when *my Bill* tells me to vote it out, I'll vote it out."

Smith laughed and said, "I love it, yer Bill's gonna love it, oh, hey, Mr. Bill, just in time."

Allen walked through the front door, Rick rolled out the Dyson bill hijack story and Allen slapped Kott a high five. Kott dropped into an overstuffed chair, put his feet on the coffee table, took a long draw off an ice-cold *Dos Equis* and yelled, "Where's the lemon?!"

Smith replied, "In the kitchen, get it yerself, do I look like yer aide?"

Kott said, "Nah, she's a lot better lookin'. Yer legs are too short and hairy, on the other hand" (a telephone rang near Allen). Kott paused and Kepner's monitor techies shook their heads as he belched, stood, scratched his crotch, and sauntered to the kitchen.

Allen picked up and said, "Hyello." It was Kohring.

"Mr. Allen, uh, Bill, say, I really need to talk to you about a, uh, relatively serious matter, uh, something important."

Allen replied, "Sure Vic, right now or can it wait till tomorrow?"

Kohring said, "As soon as possible," so Allen told him to come down to the Baranof after the floor session.

That afternoon Kohring stopped by Suite 604, grabbed a juice, scooped a handful of biscotti from the booze and hors d'oeuvres table, and sank into an overstuffed armchair. Vic took a deep breath, sighed, scrunched his brow and appealed to Allen in straightforward country humility: "Bill, uh, Mr. Allen, up on the hill they're pullin' me ten thousand different directions. I'm bushed, and I'm only here 'cause I got a personal financial matter that could hurt me politically."

Allen replied, "Yeah? What's up Vic?"

Kohring said, "I owe seventeen thousand dollars on a credit card that's in collection; they're pushin' me real hard and I don't have the money. I thought maybe you could cover me with a loan, or some work, or somethin' until..."

Kepner's people perked up, checked system status, watched, and recorded.

Rick Smith butted in, "Seventeen thousand dollars! Well yer gonna have ta keep yer mouth shut and not talk about it to anyone, especially

APOC [Alaska Public Offices Commission]. We don't need any red flags wavin' over any of us."

Kohring replied, "Yeah, I know. It's just real tough, ya know, with my wife in Portland and her mother and everyone…"

Allen interrupted the whining and said, "Rick, got any hundreds?" Smith pulled out his wallet, grabbed a fistful of bills and handed them to Allen, who handed them to Kohring, who shook Allen's hand and said, "Thanks so much, Bill. I really appreciate the help. Uh, ya know it's just real bad, what with my in-laws, and travel, and all the back and forth to Juneau. Ya know it just takes a lot of money and I'm just not sure."

Allen sighed, reached in his pocket, pulled out *another* wad of fifties and hundreds and stuffed them in Kohring's hands.

Kohring continued, "Gosh Bill, I don't know what to, what can I do at this point to help you guys? Anything?"

Allen replied, "Whatever you, you know, uh," Kohring interrupted and said, "Just keep lobbying my colleagues for the governor's plan, right?"

Allen nodded and Kohring continued, "First I'll figure out where they're at and then politely and gently, as carefully as I can, influence them in a positive way to see that the governor's bill is the vehicle they consider."

The next day Kohring called Smith and reported he had scheduled appointments with the House Finance Committee members to lobby them on the 20/20 PPT bill that VECO and the producers wanted.

Back in Anchorage, Kepner dropped a DVD into her laptop and watched as Kohring groveled for chump change. She thought about Alaska Fish and Game's recent *opener* to thin down the garbage-marauding Anchorage black bear population, shook her head and reflected on how the thrill of a hunt dissipates when the quarry proves more pathetic victim than adversary. "Black-bear dumpster diving and chump-change political handouts, they're both pathetic," she mumbled as she switched off the laptop.

———•———

Smith jolted upright from the spike of adrenaline. He looked at the fire escape, then toward the pounding at the door. With sweaty, shaking hands he quietly slipped to the door, peered through the security peephole and there stood Kott, jumping all over in excitement and pounding on the door to Suite 604. Smith jerked the door open and said, "Pete, you scared the livin' sh," Kott burst past, grabbed a beer, threw himself onto the couch and said, "We got it, man! We got it! I been working those guys and my head count puts us over the top. You're gonna get yer gas line! The governor's gonna get his bill! And I'm gonna get my job in Barbados!"

Allen got up and slapped Kott on the back. "You gotta take it easy on ol' Rick's heart, he ain't gettin' any younger, tell us about it," Allen said as he slipped the cork from a new bottle of Silver Oak, sniffed the musty-sweet end and poured a glass of Alexander Valley's finest. Kott rambled on about the momentum he'd created in the House caucus favoring the governor's *20/20* bill, who was on board, who was resisting and who was walking the fence in the majority.

As Kott was wrapping up his briefing, Allen interrupted and asked, "What about Weyhrauch? Is he okay?" Kott replied that he thought so, but wasn't sure. Allen said, "Well, he sent me a resume and a letter offering to provide legal services to VECO." Allen's neighbors strained but couldn't see the owner of a voice that warned, "Well, if you do a deal with *that* guy, don't talk about it anywhere but here." On loan from another office, Special Agent Dunphy mumbled to his partner, "Man, tell Kepner we gotta fix that blind spot. Go out and see who leaves."

As they were talking the phone rang in Suite 604. Smith picked up and said, "Boss, it's for you, Weyhrauch." Smith handed Allen the phone, "Bruce, how are ya? I got your message."

Weyrauch replied, "I just wanted to let you know I'm working on holding the line on 20/20."

Allen said, "When the session's over you need to come up and talk to me."

Weyrauch replied, "I'll do that right away."

While Allen and his shills were working the governor's *20/20* PPT in the House, the Senate was working its own modifications to the governor's bill. The Alaska senate is a twenty member body generally controlled by a narrow, eleven or twelve member Republican majority. Bill Allen wasn't too concerned about the senate "doin' the right thing," because his bases were covered by Finance Co-chair Lyda Green (the same Green who sponsored the prison split-the-baby compromise legislation), Rules Chair John Cowdery (of sinking yacht fame) and Senate President Ben Stevens, son of powerful U.S. Senator Ted Stevens and *consultant* to VECO during the legislative interim (or any other time Allen needed a little help from his friends).

Ben Stevens is a chip off the ol' block. A coarse, energetic little guy with a huge ego and flash temper, Ben is a political Yorkshire terrier bred by his dad to keep vermin under control in the Alaska senate, rather than in the mines and mills of Northern England where *Yorkies* hail from. Ben's vermin were the anti-development senate Democrats who continually gnawed at the foundation of free enterprise, stifling growth, and threatening the future of Alaska, and Ben's consulting contracts.

Ben was nine years old when his father was appointed to the United States Senate. He went to college at Arizona State, graduated with a BA in economics and went on to earn an MBA from George Washington University. He started commercial-fishing as a deck hand during college and quit fifteen years later as captain of a commercial fishing vessel. But the public really didn't hear much from or about Ben until a most extraordinary local event.

In 1998 U.S. Senator Ted Stevens had his sights on the Special Olympics 2001 Winter Games. From his post on the Senate Appropriations Committee, Senator Stevens helped steer over ten million federal dollars to site the winter competition for mentally disabled athletes in Alaska. A compassionate and empathetic son, Ben docked his Sunnfjord at Dutch Harbor, hung up his nets and crab pots, and hopped a flight to Anchorage to head up the Special Olympics efforts for his dad (and country, of course). Evidently, Ben's fifteen years of experience with bottom feeders made him the most qualified candidate for the job. But to make ends meet on the nonprofit's paltry seven hundred thousand dollar salary, Ben found it necessary to set up a consulting business on the side to help draw his influential father's attention to a variety of other worthy projects.

From 1996 to 2002, Bill Allen paid Ben two hundred twelve thousand dollars for lobbying and consulting aimed at enlisting his father's influence to resolve a contract dispute between VECO and Pakistan, as well as to secure federal funds to train VECO's Russian oil field workers. During the same period, Ben earned more than three hundred thousand dollars in consulting fees from seven offshore fishery organizations in order to secure or manage federal funds and special interest legislation important to the industry. From his seats on Senate Appropriations, and Senate Commerce, Science and Transportation, the *elder* Stevens sponsored or cosponsored (code for favor from a Senate friend) legislation and directed earmarks, or other forms of financial support favorable to his son's many business interests.

But Ben's most clever move was securing a seat on the Alaska Fisheries Marketing Board alongside elder Senator Stevens' former top Congressional Aide, Trevor McCabe. The senior Senator Stevens created the board to distribute twenty nine million dollars in federal grant funds as a "catalyst to market, develop and promote Alaska seafood" (AFMB Mission Statement). In the last week of 2002, just before the AFMB became law, Ben and Trevor started a fishing consulting company. The company, Advance North, reports accepting over seven hundred seventy five thousand dollars from nine fishing companies seeking grants from the federal funds under Ben's and Trevor's control. In a 2007 radio interview, an over-the-top, defensive Ben claimed that his father didn't appoint him to the board. He said, "I was appointed to the board by the governor, and the board members elected me chairman not my father!" It seems he forgot to mention that good ol' dad submitted his name to the governor for nomination to the board.

In 2001, Ben was appointed to fill an empty seat in the Alaska senate after Drew Pearce went to work for U.S. Interior Secretary Gale Norton. With a little help from Bill Allen and his father, Ben went on to win the seat in the fall 2002 election and was elected by his Republican peers as senate majority leader, an unprecedented honor for a freshman legislator. After a brief two year tenure as majority leader, Ben was elected president of the Alaska senate, a remarkable accomplishment that coincided nicely with Murkowski's 2006 Petroleum Production Tax bill. Funny how predictable nature can be.

PRESS RELEASE
PPT Legislation Passes Alaska Senate
(JUNEAU) April 25, 2006

Today the Alaska Senate passed Petroleum Production Tax bill (SB 305) that encourages new oil exploration and production and generates additional revenue for the state.

Senate President Ben Stevens (R-Anchorage) calls the bill a win-win for the industry and the people of Alaska. "Oil production on the North Slope is falling fast and the state needs to do all it can to halt the slide. This bill creates incentives for the major producers and independents that will eventually put more oil in the pipeline, maintain and create new job opportunities for Alaskans and generate more revenue for the state."

Ben picked up the phone, "Yeah, Bill, here's the deal: The governor wanted *20/20*. Wilkens, Dyson, Wagoner, and a couple of others in my majority wanted a twenty five percent tax and so did the minority. I couldn't risk a bi-partisan coalition vote on the floor, so I agreed to split the baby at twenty two and a half percent and raise the credit rate for capital expenditures to twenty five percent! Bill, man, you guys can drive a truck through the credit rate and recoup the 2.5% loss every year from now till kingdom come. But here's the deal. If you can hold the House at the governor's *20/20*, when we conference committee the two bills we can cut an even sweeter deal. Even if you can't hold the House, I'll squeeze their balls till they give me what I want. Let's go get a beer. Meet you in the Baranof Lounge."

Bill Allen hung up, stepped out the door of Suite 604, into the elevator and was waiting in the lounge well before Ben walked in. Gazing into his Alaskan Amber, a thoughtful Allen mused, *after he delivers the goods, ol' Ben's gonna make a real nice addition to my executive team. Hey, Ben, who's yer daddy?*

———— · ————

The House floor debate on the PPT started May 7, only two days before the end of the regular session. The debate began with sweeping partisan pontification and quickly morphed into an amendment free-for-all. Democrat Anchorage representative Harry Crawford moved to dump the profits-based tax in favor of revising the existing severance tax on gross revenue. The amendment failed. House Minority Leader Ethan Berkowitz and fellow Democrat Eric Croft (both 2006 candidates for governor) led a charge maintaining that a vote should be delayed until the governor's gas line contract was made public. Their efforts failed too.

In the early evening Weyrauch mistakenly voted the wrong way on one of a flurry of amendments which worked against VECO and the oil producers. Allen was sitting in the gallery watching the action and went nuts. He pulled out a pad, wrote a note, and caught Representative Tom Anderson looking at him. He motioned Anderson over, handed him the note and said, "Tommy, give this note to Kott. You guys gotta beat this amendment."

Anderson passed the note to Kott, who looked back and nodded. Kott went over and whispered to Weyhrauch, who turned, shrugged his shoulders and nodded his head (Weyhrauch told Allen later that a twenty one percent tax was probably a political reality, but not to worry, he'd still follow Kott's lead on the *20/20*). In the hours that followed, a wildfire of amendments were introduced to increase the production tax, followed by a *brief at ease*, followed by Anderson running notes from Allen, followed by a flurry of cell phone activity on the floor, followed by the prophetic voice of Democrat Ethan Berkowitz denouncing the improper interference from the gallery, followed by votes killing the amendments, followed by a pounding gavel announcing, "*this House is in recess to the call of the chair.*" As the beleaguered legislators filed off the floor and past the gallery, Bill Allen leaned back and smiled.

Kott winked at Allen as he passed, went out the first-floor side door and stood under an awning until Allen and Smith caught up. A splash of adrenaline, two shots of rain and a twist of euphoria carried them down the hill to the Baranof. In Suite 604 Smith poured rounds. Kott lifted his and said, "Man, I got you pointin' and passin' notes on one side and I'm lyin' in their ears on the other...we just usin' 'em and abusin' 'em. But I had to get 'er done. I had to come back and face this man right here [pointing to Allen]. I had to cheat, steal, beg, borrow, and lie to kill that sucker. Exxon's happy, BP's happy and I'll sell my soul to the devil!"

Lifting a glass to Kott, Allen laughed, leaned over, and whispered, "I own yer ass!"

The next two days were a round robin of floor debates on the pros and cons of variations on the PPT, brief *at eases*, huddles, note passing, cell-phone dialogue, votes on amendments, recesses to the *call of the chair*, closed-door caucus meetings, and *calls to order*. During a brief *at ease* on the last day of the session Weyhrauch nodded to Allen, left the floor and huddled in a corner away from reporters, staffers, and other inquiring eyes. Weyhrauch said, "Bill, I'm afraid we don't have the votes for the *20/20*. I'll follow Kott's lead, but I'm afraid a twenty one percent tax is the political reality."

Allen studied Weyhrauch's face, nodded, and said, "Well then, we'll just have to kill it and call in reinforcements during the special session. The governor's gonna keep you guys here another thirty days to ratify his contract anyway, so just run the clock and we'll kick their asses later."

Allen slipped down the hall to the senate president's office and asked if Ben was available. A couple of lobbyists were leaving and Ben waved Allen in with, "Hey Bill, how's it going in the House?"

Allen said, "I don't think we got a snowball's chance of passin' the *20/20*, and I don't trust 'em just to run the clock. My instincts tell me they're gonna pass somethin' we cain't live with. Anything you can do?"

The senate president thought for a moment and replied, "Sure, it's my way or the highway. If they won't accept the senate's deal there won't be one, cause we're not gonna compromise!"

Bill smiled at Ben and said, "How's senior vice president sound?"

———

As predicted, the Senate and House adjourned without a compromise PPT. At 11:00 a.m. the following day Governor Murkowski called the Twenty Fourth Alaska Legislature back into special session to ratify the final gas line contract and pass his 20/20 PPT legislation. Murkowski said his negotiators and consultants planned a ten day briefing on the fiscal implications, risk, economic impact and feasibility of a gas pipeline stretching from the Alaska North Slope to the midwestern United States. At 1:30 p.m. the doors to Juneau's Centennial Hall opened and a battle-weary, but curious legislature filed into the room.

It was 2006, a gubernatorial election year, and Frank Murkowski was driving the Republican Party nuts. He was the incumbent Republican and Republican incumbents just don't lose elections in Alaska. But, as one analyst observed, "Murkowski's re-election chances are deader than a shrunken head in a hackey-sack festival," and everyone knew it except Frank. So a jovial Murkowski kicked off the special session by holding up the contract documents, joking that he was going to read all nine hundred pages, starting with page one. No one laughed.

After an awkward pause, Murkowski, in his own endearing way, proceeded to threaten the legislature by reminding them that the

U.S. Department of Energy was looking into setting up a federal corporation to build the gas line and that the clock was running. He said that if the contract in his hand was not consummated, and if the state and producers didn't come to agreement, then "these issues could be taken away from us and we could lose control of the destiny of the State of Alaska."

Pete Kott looked over at House Speaker John Harris, rolled his eyes, and yawned. Murkowski spotted him and said, "What's the matter, Pete? You got a bum seat there? You want a different chair? I'd encourage all the folks in back to come in and join us in this very historic process." Well, no one can say ol' Murky is wanting in the department of hubris.

The ten-day review was an exhausting litany of projections, proposals, and permits relating to routes, risks, and rewards by international experts, economists, and ecologists. Watching the process from Anchorage on *Gavel-to-Gavel* television, a glassy-eyed Bill Allen figured he could occupy his time more productively by sending personal e-mails to select members of the majority, asking each to vote for the 20% PPT bill introduced by the governor. At Centennial Hall an equally attentive Representative Weyhrauch checked his laptop, spotted the message, hit *reply*, typed, "I will be arriving in Anchorage on Wednesday May 24 and would like to meet with you at 4 pm to discuss a mutually beneficial relationship," and clicked *send*.

When Allen checked his *inbox*, Rick Smith happened to be sitting across the desk. Bill read the e-mail to Rick and said, "How do you think we should handle him?"

Rick replied, "He's not worth anything to us unless he votes our way and brings others with him. Why don't we string him out for a while until he produces?"

Allen nodded, looked out the bronze executive windows at a glistening snowfield high in the Chugach Range and said, "Let's have dinner with him tonight, get his commitment, tell him we'll help him out, and let it go at that. He'll do what he can and we'll do what we need to, if he produces."

The dinner went as expected. But both Bill and Rick were pleasantly surprised when Weyhrauch confessed and belabored the fact that he wasn't doing so well financially. "Shades of Kohring," Allen thought to himself. The next day Smith assured a concerned ConocoPhillips lobbyist that the relationship with Weyhrauch was going well and VECO was "keeping him in a good place."

Smith smiled and said, "Bruce will be good." Smith's phone rang again. This time it was Kott calling from Juneau.

"Pete," Smith said, "how're ya doin' pardner?"

Kott answered, "Hey, how many of them hats you want CBC on the back of?"

Smith frowned and replied, "Excuse me?"

Kott said, "CBC. How many hats?"

The light dawned on Smith, who laughed and replied, "*The Corrupt Bastards Club*! Oh, I don't know, fifteen or twenty of 'em."

"Yeah, that's what I thought," said Kott, "next we gotta figure out who the club is."

Smith said, "You'll figure it out. By the way I gave Bill the *'Git 'Er Done'* hat, too, and he loved it. I gotta get to work on the Murkowski fundraiser, so I'll see you back in Juneau in a couple of days."

"Okay," Kott replied, "hey, transfer me over to the boss," and waited.

Allen picked up, "Hello?"

Kott shouted, "Uncle Bill!"

A surprised Allen answered, "Hey Pete, what in hell ya doin?"

Kott said, "I'm waitin' on yer ass."

Allen replied, "I'll be there tomorrow, right after the fundraiser."

Kott offered, "that's good, because we're probably gonna have PPT on the floor on Friday, and hey, ah, you remember those pills you gave me?"

Allen said, "Yeah."

Kott went on, "Man, I been havin' a hard time sleepin'. I took one of 'em last night. Every time I turned over I rolled over on my projection."

Allen laughed and said, "So they worked pretty good, huh?"

Kott groaned and said, "No, kept me awake all night! Every time I'd roll over man, I was like, never mine, I just need to know which one's er which?"

Between tears and laughter Allen choked out a reply, "I told ya, the little white one's fer sex and the brown one's fer sleep'n."

Kott yelled back, "I took the wrong ones, no wonder I couldn't sleep!"

Gasping and soar from laughter Allen asked, "Well, what'd yer ol' lady think about it?"

Kott said, "She took the other one and passed out like a drunken sailor and I laid awake all night at full alert."

Tears rolling down his cheeks, Allen caught his breath and said, "You're something else, Pete. See ya tomorrow."

The special-session floor debates resumed after the gas line contract briefings and Smith and Allen returned to Suite 604. On May 30, 2006, Weyhrauch sent a handwritten note to Allen on legislative letterhead saying, "It was great to finally spend some time with you and Rick last week. Call any time. I look forward to working with you and VECO in the future."

Allen opened the envelope the next day, smiled, folded the note and laid it on an end table thinking, "I rope his head, Rick gets his heels, and we corral another one, jest like rodeoin' without the saddle sores." A knock on the door interrupted Allen's reflection and he yelled, "Come on in!" The door opened and Kott walked in with a big smile.

Kott gave Allen a rundown on the majority caucus meeting, said nothing much was going on and he just dropped by to say hi. Allen said he appreciated Kott's work and handed him a thousand dollars in cash. Kott stuffed the bills into his politically incorrect Carharts and Allen said, "There, that should keep you in broads and booze for a couple days."

Kott grinned and said, "Ya know, I been thinkin'. When we get this deal, instead of Barbados warden, I'd like to hang up my CBC cap and lobby for you guys."

Allen looked at Kott, grinned, and replied, "Well, you will be. Let's go get some grub."

Over the next week, the Governor's *20/20* PPT bill took a beating in the House with Democrats and renegade Republicans forming what appeared to be a *perfect storm* of votes to raise the tax. The only real squabble in the House seemed to be how high, and the numbers weren't pretty. On June sixth, the House suddenly bumped the bill from the governor's twenty percent to twenty three and a half percent, and all hell broke loose among the oil industry lobbyists. When Bill Allen heard the news he called ConocoPhillips' Alaska president Jim Bowles to talk strategy.

"Jim, this here's Bill Allen, and we got a problem." Allen told Bowles about the hike and said, "We wanna just see if we can't stop this thing, don't we, Jim?"

Bowles replied, "Yes, sir. If there's any way we can get this thing stopped, that's the best possible outcome."

Allen nodded and said, "Okay, well, I got workin', and it's just between me and you, I got Pete Kott and, uh, Ben doin' it and hopefully we can, they're gonna try."

Bowles thought for a moment and said, "Well, Bill, one thing I think we had talked about is that probably the best outcome for us is to get the House to go ahead and gavel out and finish up and get them out of town."

"Right, that's what I'm tryin' to do," Allen replied, but Bowels interrupted, "If we can get them out of town, we've got a better chance. Then all we've got to do is just work the senate by themselves."

Allen continued, "You know, I think the problem is the damn Governor is flippin' to twenty two and a half percent."

Bowles frowned and said, "Well, that's not a good answer..." Allen jumps in "Jim, I know, I know, if we can't shut down then he may call another special session real quick."

"Well, we can deal with that next," Bowles replied. "We met with the Governor yesterday and we told him twenty two and a half percent is not good. We'd actually prefer twenty three and a half because it provides the basis to say we've got a terrible result. Bill, I think if we can get this killed this time, we can come back and package up something that works better for the Governor and for ourselves."

Allen "uh huh'd" and said, "It's not one hundred percent, probably we got an eighty percent chance of getting the House shut down."

Bowles paused and said, "That would be good. So we'll stay in touch. Thanks for the call, Bill."

Allen replied, "You bet. Bye."

Disgusted and with two days to go, Kott, Weyrauch, Smith, Allen, and Ben Stevens pushed for adjournment before votes could be taken on an amended bill that VECO and the producers couldn't support. The adjournment plan failed, but the group leveraged enough support to run the clock on the debate and on June 8, 2006, the legislature adjourned, failing again to pass the 20/20 Petroleum Production Tax bill. The next morning Allen left Bowles a voicemail message, "Hey Jim, I told you we would, uh, between Pete Kott and with Ben we wouldn't have a bill. So I know you're probably talkin' with someone else. But remember what I told you, that we got 'er done!"

———•———

Two weeks after the special session Governor Murkowski issued an

Executive Proclamation scheduling another thirty day special session beginning July 12, 2006. The focus of the special session was, again, the governor's proposed 20/20 PPT bill and the gas line contract. Cranky legislators whined that the special sessions were cutting into campaigns and fundraising in an election year. The whimpering had no effect on Murkowski, who had shocked the state a week before by announcing that he was, indeed, running for a second term. Evidently something in a twenty thousand dollar secret poll gave Murkowski some cause for optimism. The fact that the poll was requested by Jim Clark, Murkowski's chief of staff, and paid for by Rick Smith from VECO funds would prove to be a bit of a federal *conspiracy to commit fraud* problem for Clark and others at a future date.

In the days leading up to the July special session Bill and Rick kept real busy illegally commissioning and paying for political consultants and polls for Clark, Kott, and Stevens, dangling *consulting* bait in front of Weyhrauch, serving as Kohring's drive-by cash ATM, crafting a foolproof plan to funnel $8,000 into Kott's bank account through bogus billings, and meeting with Ben Stevens about his new executive position with VECO, to be announced, of course, after the special sessions. Nonetheless, Bill and Rick were still concerned over having enough votes, so Cowdery set up a breakfast meeting with Allen and Senator Donny Olson to broker a favorable PPT vote in exchange for a bargain twenty five thousand dollars in campaign *contributions* to Olson's upcoming campaign. The breakfast dialogue was the recorded subject of Cowdery's later indictments for bribery and conspiracy to commit extortion.

In the end, Murkowski, the producers, VECO and its small army of well-positioned shills couldn't muster the juice to force-feed the legislature the *20/20* PPT. On August 10, 2006, the legislature passed one of the most significant pieces of legislation in Alaska state history, replacing the outdated Economic Limit Factor (ELF) with a new "profits-based" Petroleum Production Tax of *22.5%* on net positive cash flow, and *20%* credit on oil and gas investment. The following year the new PPT generated nearly two million dollars additional revenue for the State of Alaska…right out of the major producers' pockets.

———————

"You wanna 'nother one, Rick?" Smith squinted up at the Buckaroo

Club bartender and said, "Yeah, hit me, Pardner, it was a longg session. I been rid hard, put up wet and gotta climb back on tomorrow out at Moose Run."

Charlie Buckner looked up and down the dark, pretty much empty bar and whispered, "Young?" Rick looked around and said, "Yeah, he flew in from DC last week for his annual cash hump. Just finished the Pork Roast fundraiser, did pretty good, around forty five thousand. We're doin' the golf thang tomorrow, then I'm done till someone else needs money."

Charlie nodded and said, "You be needin' cash?" Rick smiled. "Got a few checks if you don't mind cashin'em for me ol' buddy. It'll save me a trip to the bank."

Charlie shook his head and said, "Ya know Rick, someone's gonna catch up with you one uh these days."

Rick gazed into his amber scotch and said, "Nah, I doubt it. Moose Run's just a bunch of good ol' boys; a private game, some winners, some losers, you know."

Charlie opened the till and said, "How much *prize money* you got in mind? I might need to go to the back room."

Rick pulled out an envelope and said, "I don't know. I think I got around twenty, maybe twenty five grand in checks. Here, you count 'em."

The Buckaroo Club is a quiet country bar in the Spenard area of Anchorage, a couple blocks south of Chilkoot Charlie's, *"where we cheat the other guy and pass the savings on to you."* When Rick was tired, or needed to take care of a little business, he preferred the Buckaroo's dark, laid-back done yer momma wrong, cryin' in yer beer, two-steppin' nostalgia to *Koot's* six-bar, beer'n-shots, fur-bikini, pole-slidin', mud-wrestlin', grunge'n- roll, twenty-somethin' party crowd…though the locally trapped fur bikinis do add a warm frontier touch. An added amenity was the club's proximity to a number of psychic massage, escort, and gaming services where, after an uplifting palm reading a guy could relax, share the day's burden with an understanding therapist, and stroll into a stimulating game of chance.

Kepner stretched, looked out the window, and thought, "Great day for golf!" The Moose Run golf course is located across town on the Fort Richardson military base and Kepner needed about an hour to organize her gear and set up. After a quick bite she threw her equipment in an SUV and headed west under a group of ravens gliding down from the Chugach Range for a day of dumpster diving and tourist handouts. At the entrance to the base a sharp-eyed security officer spotted the discreet identifier on the plate and waved her through the gate. A couple of miles later Kepner pulled into a gravel lot, parked, put on her *Nike Summer Lites,* unfolded the cart, and wheeled over to a picnic table in front of the Moose Run clubhouse.

Adjusting the golf cart elbow for audio and video, Kepner scanned her surroundings. Directly in front lay a long, narrow, slightly dog-legged emerald green fairway. Off to the right, splashing, sparkling, and all full of herself, Ship Creek meandered between parallel ninth and tenth holes tickled on both shoulders by long, sensuous fingers of weeping birch. On the left, at the bottom of a slight grade, Kepner could just make out a familiar figure. "Chad. How many you got?" she whispered.

She saw Chad casually glance around, tip his head slightly, and speak clearly into her left ear. "I'm thinkin' two dozen players. How 'bout you?"

Kepner replied, "Yeah, that's my take, not counting Smith and the congressman."

At that instant a large shadow eclipsed Kepner's own on the picnic table. She stiffened, turned into the sun and squinted up to see who was standing behind her.

A voice rang out, "Mary Beth, I thought that was you!"

Eyes darting in both directions Kepner quietly said, "Your honor, I mean, uh, Judge Sedwick, gee, great to see you." Kepner stood, shook the judge's hand, leaned forward, and whispered, "I'm working."

Sedwick frowned and replied, "What? Ohhhh, well, uh, great, great to see you," tipped his golf cap, turned and ambled off toward the clubhouse. Kepner sat down, shook her head, and snickered, thinking, "Alaska *is* a small town." "Chad. Are you there? You're not gonna believe this."

The event turned out to be the same as previous years. A bunch of Anchorage business types and lobbyists wrote checks to Rick Smith to cover *the expenses* of an informal golf get-together honoring their ol' buddy Congressman Young. After nine holes everyone gathered at the watering hole, where Rick Smith handed out a few preliminary door prizes for a variety of accomplishments like Lowest Score, Longest Drive, Oldest Duffer, and Happy Hooker. After a few more rounds (of drinks), Rick announced the grand prize lottery drawing. As the crowd hushed in suspense, Rick pulled a number out of a hat and announced that lucky ol' leprechaun Don Young won *again* this year. While the crowd laughed and whistled, Congressman Young stepped forward to collect his prize and say a few words of appreciation.

After a very few words, Smith grabbed the mike, toasted the terrific day of golf, handed Young an unmarked envelope stuffed with cash and told everyone, "Party on dudes!" Young slipped the bulging envelope into a pocket and made the rounds, greeting his good friends and supporters. The only difference this year was that Don and Rick didn't recognize a couple of the guests, one even got some great pictures to share with them at a more formal future event.

With the golf tournament recorded and the legislature dealing its final hand on the petroleum production tax, Kepner prepared to play her hand. The phone at my desk rang. I glanced at the caller identification, recognized Kepner's private cell phone and picked up. "Hi Mary Beth, what's going on?" I asked.

"Listen," she said, "remember our talk about Senator Dyson?" I said I did. "Do you think you could reach out to him and set up a meeting with me?" I said I could and asked when and where? Kepner answered, "Anytime this week, but the sooner the better. My office is fine, unless he'd feel more comfortable somewhere else. Just let me know, and thanks, Frank, we're about to go overt and couldn't have got here without you. I'll brief you later." We hung up and I called Dyson.

I first met Fred Dyson in 1975. He was an engineer of some kind for British Petroleum. I always suspected the North Slope oil work gave him the wages and schedule to pursue one of his other peculiar passions: picking up strays (of the human variety) and introducing them to the practical, rather than the religious, side of Jesus. Truthfully, Fred has a lot in common with the radical revolutionary who set convention upside down a couple thousand years ago. During the late '60s Fred could be found at U.C. Berkeley standing on a step in Sproul Plaza, captivating crowds of students with the notion that the sociopolitical change advocated by his friends Mario Savio and the SDS (at the other end of the plaza) was only a Band Aid on a festering, infected, national wound. Fred argued that institutions are made up of people, and the only way to change sociopolitical convention is to radically change the hearts of people. He harbored the same feelings about religious convention.

In the thirty years I've known them, Fred and his wife, Jane, have walked their talk, feeding and housing the poor, raising abandoned and abused children, lending a hand to neighbors, and resisting the natural impulses of political payback and power politics. Kepner had asked earlier if I knew anyone inside the legislature she could trust, "Someone honest and smart, with good observation skills, keen instincts, and discretion." Now if you've ever spent any time in politics, you might think that was a trick question. But I knew immediately Fred was the guy.

So on a calm and sunny afternoon I called Fred. "Misty Dancer, Misty Dancer, this is Orca, over." I repeated the call a couple of times, pausing each time for a response when I heard a crackly, "Orca, this is Misty Dancer, down two to one-four." I switched channels on my VHF radio as Fred replied, "Greetings, brother. Where you at?" I told him that Vicki and I were sailing north up Port Wells, toward College Fjord. Fred replied that he was across the channel at Granite Bay, so we agreed to raft up at Hobo Bay.

Hobo Bay sits near the entrance to College Fjord in remote western Prince William Sound. The fjord is a spectacular arm of mountains rising from sea level three thousand vertical feet into the crisp Alaska air. Nestled in between the steep granite canyons' cracks and crevices are twenty eight breathtaking glaciers which calve great chunks of sapphire-blue ice into the silty water below. On the outgoing tide, chattering congregations of kittiwake and sleepy-eyed harbor seal flip and flap their way aboard the great chunks of ice, preening and basking their way down the channel like cruise ship tourists soaking up the midnight summer sun.

Granite Bay is one of Fred's favorite summer haunts, so I figured I could raise him by radio if I just headed north out of Whittier Harbor after rounding Pigot Point. My wife and I were already at anchor when Fred idled into the bay at the fly bridge of his converted aluminum-hull Bristol Bay sternpicker. Fred pulled alongside, snugged up against our fenders, and Vicki tossed Jane a couple of dock lines to secure their boat to ours. Fred shut down his engines and yelled, "Permission to come aboard!?" My wife and I waved them over for some BB King, smoked Copper River red salmon and a glass of Pinot Gris.

Over the next couple of hours I told Fred the whole saga of our adventure with the FBI and the apocalyptic events that were likely to unfold.

Fred, being Fred, listened quietly, gazed across the sparkling clear bay, turned to me with furrowed brow and a hint of a tear and said, "I love you, brother. Are you guys okay?"

I assured him Vicki and I were fine, but it had been a long and stressful journey. "More important, Fred," I said, "this thing has gone further than anyone ever expected, and it seems to be getting bigger every day. I don't think it's going to stop until it reaches the governor and our congressional delegation. The political implications are huge."

Fred whistled, acknowledged he'd be happy to meet with Kepner and said, "Let's see if we can catch us some dinner. I'm starvin'."

A week later Senator Dyson called Bill Allen and said, "Bill. Dyson. Let's get together for breakfast and talk about the session."

Allen shifted his cell phone to his good ear and replied, "Sure, that'd be great, Fred. When and where?"

Dyson said, "How about tomorrow morning at the Kodiak Café. I'll pick you up." Allen suggested around 8:00 a.m. Dyson said that would be great and hung up.

The next morning Dyson stuck a recording device in his pocket, picked Allen up at VECO headquarters and headed downtown. The Kodiak Café is on Fourth avenue, across the street from an Office Depot and the Anchorage regional office of the Federal Bureau of Investigation. When Dyson pulled up to a vacant curbside meter he looked in his rearview mirror and saw a beige Taurus pull up behind him. Allen was taking off his seatbelt and getting ready to open the door when Dyson put his hand on Allen's knee and said, "Bill, I've always considered you a friend. There's some people behind us who want to talk with you, but only if you're willing. They're federal agents and wanna talk about your relationship with the legislature. I've seen some of their concerns and my advice is to hear them out. You don't have to say a thing. Just listen to them."

A stunned Allen opened the door and stepped out onto the sidewalk. "Mr. Allen, I'm Special Agent Mary Beth Kepner with the FBI. Our office is right behind you. Would you mind meeting with us? We'd like to show you some things." Allen hesitated and Kepner interjected, "If you want an attorney we'd be happy to wait. Why don't we just get off the street and you can think about it inside." Allen nodded and followed Kepner to the electric side gate. Two more agents materialized and followed them into the building. A fourth agent stuck his head into Dyson's car, thanked him for the help and asked for the recording device.

A troubled and conflicted Dyson looked over at the Kodiak Café, fired up his truck and headed down to the Legislative Information Office for a Health and Social Service subcommittee teleconference.

Chapter Five

Play Ball!

Associated Press
Wednesday, Aug. 23, 2006
Anchorage, Alaska

Republican Gov. Frank Murkowski, stung by accusations of arrogance and stubbornness, lost his bid for a second term Tuesday after polling last in a three-way GOP primary. Murkowski, 73, sought to make the primary a referendum on his proposal to build a $25 billion natural gas pipeline to Canada. His approval ratings have skidded over the past four years because of much-criticized decisions such as appointing his daughter to his U.S. Senate seat and purchasing a state jet after his request was denied by the state legislature. Murkowski polled just 19 percent of the vote.

When a major investigation moves from covert to overt, the primary focus becomes to expeditiously accomplish the mission at hand, but assessing the foreseeable spinoff when the case goes public is of equal importance. Kepner was busy plotting where the rats would scurry after she lifted the lid. She wasn't paying much attention to the primary election until I called her and said, "Kepner, have you seen the ad?"

She replied, "What ad?"

"Frank Murkowski's full page *mea culpa* in the Anchorage Daily News this morning, you're gonna love it," I said.

In a desperate attempt to drive his popularity polls into double digits, Murkowski was running full-page newspaper ads where, through a cheesy smile, he told Alaskans, *"I agree. I admit it. I'm a long, long way from perfect. At one time or another, I've made nearly the entire state of Alaska mad at me. Maybe I should consider a personality transplant. But in Alaska, sometimes it takes a strong will to make things happen..."* Murkowski couldn't have put his finger on the problem better if he'd said it himself. And former Miss Wasilla-mayor-hockey-mom Sarah Palin was there to take Frank to the bank. The "politically inexperienced" Palin built her platform on transparency in government and ethics. Craftily catching the Republican Party establishment with their ethical pants down, Palin went on to win a populace referendum in the general election capitalizing on the impending FBI investigations into Alaska political corruption and delivering the shell-shocked populace a message it evidently wanted to hear.

Kepner finished reading the ad and called me back. "Frank," she said, "Great ad. By the way, I'm gonna be out-of-pocket at Regional Headquarters for a few days. If anything comes up on your end, give Chad a call. If I don't see you before this weekend, make sure you keep a close eye on the news."

———

Federal Bureau of Investigations regional headquarters in Anchorage is a rectangular, red brick, two-story building that takes up a full city block. The walls at street level contain no windows, one discreet public entrance, and a large electric gate that quietly regulates a steady flow of vehicles to and from the bowels of the building. Most of the activity occurs on the second floor, where a maze of perimeter offices surround two huge, glass-wall, natural-skylight, conference rooms. The exterior office windows are smokey, one-way glass, allowing no visual penetration from without. Ironically, for years the view from *less costly* Bill Weimar's executive suite faced the FBI building across the street. Weimar would periodically meet with compromised public officials in his office, and after swapping expectations, look out the window at the FBI building, lean into his desk lamp and whisper, *but we wouldn't do that, because that would be wrong.*

At seven a.m. on August 31, 2006, the FBI building was a beehive of activity. Both conference rooms were jammed with local agents, loaner

"TDY" agents from other regions, computer technicians, forensic specialists, U.S. attorneys and administrative assistants. Easels and white boards surrounded the perimeter of the rooms, displaying a textured collage of aerial photos, maps, interior diagrams, exterior pictures, timelines, and targets.

Multiple copies of twenty independent search warrants were laid out on a large conference table with detailed instructions for locating the evidence described in the text. Signed late the previous evening, the warrants authorized the search and seizure "...from a period of October 2005 to the present, of any and all documents, reflecting or relating to proposed legislation in the state of Alaska involving either the creation of a natural gas pipeline or the petroleum production tax." They also authorized seizing any evidence "relating to any payment" to lawmakers by VECO executives and "any physical garments (including hats) bearing any of the following logos or phrases: CBC, Corrupt Bastards Club, Corrupt Bastards Caucus, VECO."

By eleven a.m. federal agents and support staff were positioned outside VECO headquarters in Anchorage, as well as the Anchorage, Juneau, Nome, Eagle River and Wasilla offices of Alaska representatives Kott, Kohring, and Weyhrauch and Alaska senators Cowdery, Stevens, and Olson, as well as an undisclosed location in Girdwood (a ski resort thirty miles South of Anchorage where, coincidentally, U.S. senator Ted Stevens maintains his Alaska residence). With every team in position Kepner gave *Operation Dirt Ball* the green light and federal agents throughout Alaska swarmed into history in an unprecedented exercise of sovereign federal police power over a state legislative body.

For two days badge-dangling federal agents, technicians, and support staff could be seen entering and leaving the state capitol building, legislative offices, and VECO headquarters with file boxes, artifacts, daypacks, cameras, portable scanners, and a variety of plastic containers labeled with each office and person of interest. In an uncharacteristically prescient moment, a visibly stunned Cowdery turned to a loitering reporter and volunteered, "I'm not worried about my *indictment*." Self-fulfilling prophesy can be such a bother.

When the cat was finally released from the bag, it predictably dragged along an exponential increase in Kepner's workload. Except for bum-ming an occasional free meal, or periodic calls asking whether I understood the significance of this, or that, or remembered how one or another thing occurred, I didn't see much of Kepner during September and October of 2006. Kepner and a small army of Justice Department officials were terribly busy conducting interviews and sifting through a mountain of seized documents and records, tracing and connecting cause-and-effect relations to questionable results, results that led to more interviews, which led to more sources, which were then traced for cause-and-effect relations that led to more questionable results until finally, the prize: a federal crime. And crimes there were a plenty, a veritable cornucopia of corruption flowing out the door of Suite 604, transforming official acts into crimes and overflowing into the perverse pockets of bought and paid-for politicians.

Except for a follow-up raid seizing "all records" relating to Senator Ben Stevens' involvement with Alaska fisheries, and Lesil McGuire's remarkable ascension to the Alaska senate, only one other event of note wrapped up the year. At four p.m. on December 7, 2006, Kepner turned her sedan into a driveway on Kimberly Lyn Circle in the Bayshore area of South Anchorage. The subdivision is an unpretentious collection of new, vaulted-ceiling, cookie-cutter, two-story homes on postage-stamp lots surrounded by a spruce swamp and partial view of the Chugach Mountains. Kepner and her partner, Special Agent Chad Joy, walked up to the door and rang the bell. In a few seconds the door opened. Tom Anderson looked at Kepner and Joy and, with a big smile said, "Hey guys, how are ya? Long time no see. Arrest any bad guys lately?"

Chad looked at Anderson and said, "Nope. You're *the first*. Turn around and put your hands behind your back."

Still grinning, Anderson said, "Yeah, heh-heh, right. Come on, what can I do for you two? *Really*, it's nice to see ya."

Chad replied, "Tom, *really*, do what I said." A flash of concern crossed Anderson's face. He hesitated, looked at Kepner, turned, put his hands behind his back and shivered as ice cold steel snapped around his wrists with a ratcheting noise that sliced the crisp winter air. Kepner took Anderson's arm, led him to the sedan, opened a rear door and herded him into the back seat. Agent Joy slipped in beside him as Kepner started the car and pulled out of the driveway.

Looking in the rearview mirror Kepner caught Anderson's eye and asked, "Well, Tom, do you have anything to say?"

Anderson, looking out the car window at a puzzled neighbor staring out her living room window, shook his head and quietly said, "I guess I just had too many masters."

Anderson was booked into the Anchorage jail as an overhead TV news monitor announced Alaska's first finalist for *America's Biggest Loser*. He appeared in federal court the next morning wearing a bright yellow jumpsuit with the word *PRISONER* stenciled across his back. When the clerk of the court said, "All rise," Anderson's leg irons jangled as he stood to watch the federal magistrate enter the room.

"Thomas T. Anderson?" the magistrate asked, looking Anderson in the eye.

"Yes, your honor," Anderson replied.

"Please be seated," the magistrate said, scanning the documents in front of him. "Mr. Anderson, you're charged with two counts of extortion, one count of bribery, one count of conspiracy, and three counts of money laundering in connection with the use of a sham corporation to hide the identity of bribery payments." Looking up, the magistrate asked, "Do you have an attorney?"

Anderson hesitated a moment and said, "Yes, sir."

"Have you discussed the charges with him?" the magistrate asked.

"Yes, sir," Anderson replied.

"Then how do you plead?" the magistrate inquired.

"Not guilty, sir," Anderson said.

In a written statement Senator-Elect Lesil McGuire said, "We're just devastated by the events. He feels there have been grave misunderstandings in all of this and is anxious to tell his side of the story." Asked how *she* felt, McGuire assured her constituents that she was not the target of any investigation and the events occurred well before she actually married Anderson, who was just "low hanging fruit" in the greater federal investigation. I put down the paper and reached for my coffee, humming "*There she goes just a walkin' down the street, sing'n doo wadiidy diddy doo diddy dumb* and thought, Senator *Lethal* McGuire, what a catch."

The day the indictment was made public, the *Anchorage Daily News* pieced together enough information to blow my cover. Kepner had warned me about the impending arrest and possibility of exposure, but she didn't realize the indictment was so in-artfully crafted that CS-1 could be only one of three people, so I issued an affirming statement to the press to protect my two old friends and business associates.

The next morning my phone rang early. It was my older daughter, Tara. "Is this CS-1? Holy crap, Dad, you're all over the paper, what are you thinking!? What's going on?"

I replied, "Hi, honey, it's uh, just a little project I've been working on. I'll fill you in later, but I'm kind of in a hurry. Don't worry, I'm okay."

Tara asked if I was sure, said she'd *definitely* catch me later, and hung up mumbling something about relief over her new married name and her Dad, *Secret Agent Man.*

Relying on the detailed indictment, the *Anchorage Daily News* reported that the criminal conspiracy between Anderson and "Lobbyist A" began in July 2004 and continued through March 2005. They reported that Lobbyist A set up a shell company called Pacific Publishing, which existed solely to launder money to Anderson. "CS-1" paid "Lobbyist A" twenty four thousand dollars for bogus advertising that was then pocketed by Anderson and "Lobbyist A." The reporter said that the identity of "CS-1" closely matched Frank Prewitt, a former corrections commissioner appointed by Governor Wally Hickel, and disclosed that *In an e-mail exchange with the Daily News on Friday, Prewitt suggested he was the source, though he stopped short of confirming it. He wrote, 'at this time it is inappropriate for me to talk about the voluntary role I and others may have played in the Anderson investigation. Over the next year I believe you will find that this was only the beginning of the end of a sad, but healthy chapter in Alaska history. My prayers are with Representative Anderson and his family during this difficult time for all.'*

Cover blown, life for CS-1 (code name *Patient*) would never be the same.

On New Year's Day 2007, in the true spirit of the Last Frontier, Almost-Attorney-Senator-Elect Lesil McGuire determined her first official act of the New Year would be to show support for her newly O.R. *(own recognizance)* released, stay-at-home husband, *former* Representative Tom Anderson. Lesil was in the lobby of the Anchorage Captain Cook Hotel when she decided to call Tom's co-conspirator, Bill Bobrick. Bobrick was walking his old poodle, Archie, on the Anchorage Coastal Trail when his cell phone rang. He said, "Hello?" and a female voice immediately replied, "Are you recording this?" Bobrick recognized Lesil McGuire's voice and assured her that he wasn't. McGuire identified herself and said, "Your wife needs to know some things that could affect her ability to get her medical license." Bobrick listened for a bit and then told her he was walking his dog and would call her back.

Bobrick immediately dialed Kepner, "Mary Beth?" Kepner responded, "Yes, Bill, what's up?"

Bobrick said, "I hate to bother you on New Year's, but I just got a very disturbing call from Lesil McGuire. Everyone knows my wife is in med school and plans to practice in Anchorage. I think she's trying to threaten me because she's figured out I'll be testifying against Tom. What should I do?"

Kepner thought for a moment and replied, "Call her back when you get home and record the conversation. Just listen and thank her for the heads up. Then call me back." They hung up and Kepner thought, "Witness tampering. How dumb can she get!?"

When Bobrick got home the red light on his message machine was blinking. He pushed *play* and there was Lesil, again, "Hello, uh, if anyone's listening to this recording, I have a feeling you're required to report who called here but I'm not in that category. I'm calling on a personal matter about your wife. I left her a message but would like to talk to you about it. It's very disturbing and could impact her. What this person said was not kind, it was awful, and they made an implication that could affect her potential medical career." Bobrick called his wife, who confirmed that she had received a weird and disturbing message from Lesil saying there were people out to get her.

Bobrick called Kepner, who called U.S. Attorney Joe Bottini, who called Tom Anderson's lawyer, Paul Stoeckler and said, "Paul, get a handle on your client's wife and explain to them threatening or tampering with a federal witness is a felony. And we're damn serious about it!" Stoeckler shook his head, groaned, assured Bottini it would not happen again and called his client. "Tom, what are you guys thinking!?" Anderson assured Stoeckler it was all just a big misunderstanding and they wouldn't call again. Stoeckler then called Bottini, who called Kepner, who called Bobrick to assure him everything would be just fine. Kepner hung up the phone, shook her head, looked at her friends' puzzled New Year's Day expressions and said, "It was nothing. As one of my sources puts it, just a little problem with *Lethal* McGuire." Everyone laughed, rolled their eyes and went back to the game.

Alaska State of the State
January 17, 2007
Governor Sarah Palin

Good evening. It is an honor to stand before you tonight…my
Alaskan family. My administration reflects new people with
new ideas inspired to find new ways of governing…and we're
filled with boundless new energy.

I say to you tonight that the state of the State is strong. It is
promising, but without increased oil development forecasts
show a 100 million dollar reduction each year in revenue. It
is time to ramp up responsible resource development. Frankly,
I'm struck by the absurd situation we are in…a state so blessed
with energy resources, yet many communities face threats to
safety and well being because of the high price and limited
supply of energy.

I respond to this challenge in three words: NATURAL GAS
PIPELINE! This pipeline will fuel our homes, our economy
and careers for Alaskans for generations. It's critical not just
for our future, but the Nation's future. Bringing that gas to
market is costly and risky, but there's no question…this is
sound economic development.

Over the last year Alaskans have learned a lot from the prior attempt to develop our gas under the old 'Stranded Gas Development Act.' I'm here to tell you Alaska's gas is not stranded! It's
time we leave the Stranded Gas Development Act in the past
and move forward with a new vehicle. My cabinet is develop-
ing a bill entitled the Alaska Gasline Inducement Act, 'AGIA.'
My intent is not to take the Producers' word for marketability,
but to INDUCE them to build, or sell gas to someone else who
builds a gas pipeline.

In addition to AGIA, we intend to ask the Legislature to review the new Petroleum Profits Tax passed during the last

legislative session. I would have preferred sticking with our proven method of taxing oil and gas based on its gross value, rather than an oil company's 'claimed' expenses and profits. But that's now the law, so we'll watch carefully as the first tax returns come in to make sure there aren't any surprises…and if there are, lets try again and get it right!

My mission is putting Alaskans first by restoring trust, controlling spending and communication between the people's government and the people. Just as the public placed its trust in me, I place my trust in all of you!

May God bless us and this great State.

Kepner turned off her television. Looking at her husband she said, "When the indictments come down this spring, I think we may be looking at another special session. The governor doesn't like the PPT and she's gonna like it a lot less when she smells the stench that surrounded the debate!"

———

The toxic free radicals introduced into the 2007 Legislative body by its infected members altered the molecular structure of the Alaska House and Senate, creating an unstable air of uncertainty and distrust. In a made-for-television tantrum over being refused the senate presidency, startled Republicans watched as Republican senator Lyda Green jumped ship with a handful of Republican mutineers and sold their partisan loyalties to Democrats, in exchange for the president, majority leader and rules chair. In return, for the first time in fifteen years senate Democrats held key committee chairmanships and a coalition majority. They called themselves the *Senate Bipartisan Working Group*. Stunned and disgusted, the estranged remnants of the former Republican majority reorganized as the *Senate Moral Minority* and quietly watched as the spoils of political betrayal were distributed to a grinning former Democrat senate minority.

To complicate matters, the new *transparent* Republican governor was polling an unprecedented 88% public approval rating by embracing fair and open dialogue, while strong-arming partisan Republican old guard attempts to control the political agenda. The only question was whether she had substance and leadership ability. It was just too soon to tell whether Palin (unlike Murkowski) was just another pretty face. So, with no clear executive branch leadership and two deeply divided legislative bodies, very little occurred during 2007, until April, when Agent Kepner flew to Juneau to make some house calls.

———

KTUU - Bill McAllister
Monday, April 23, 2007
JUNEAU, Alaska

A happy ending to a long Coast Guard search as former state Legislator Bruce Weyhrauch, 54, is alive tonight and in stable condition in Juneau.

There was a feeling of dread in the Capitol this morning, as former Rep. Weyhrauch had been missing since 6:30 pm Sunday. But this story has a near-miracle ending. The Juneau attorney went out salmon fishing about 5 pm Sunday on his 14-foot Boston Whaler. The Coast Guard said someone spotted the boat running with nobody on board and adrift at 6:30 pm. Weyrauch fell out of his boat and spent an hour in the 40 degree water before paddling his way to Coughlan Island where he spend a rainy, mosquito infested night. He was found this morning by the Sea Dogs, a volunteer canine unit under the direction of the Troopers.

It was an electric moment on the House floor when Majority Leader Ralph Samuels, R-Anchorage, made the announcement this morning that Weyhrauch was safe.

After reading the article I picked up the phone and dialed Kepner. "Hey, you better start arresting some of these guys before they die of old age or start jumping out of boats," I chuckled.

Kepner answered, "Not funny. We were really concerned. I talked to him about things on Friday. Don't know for sure, but I'm thinkin' pickin' up soap bars off the floor of a federal pen wasn't what he had planned. Just wait till next week." I tried to pry more information out of her, but FBI agents are very good at answering questions without saying anything so I gave up and wished her good hunting. After all, Juneau is a hunters' paradise and I could tell from her evasive manner that Kepner had spotted fresh tracks and steaming scat.

On May 4, 2007, after a hearty Baranof breakfast, Kepner and her small band of merry agents split up and scooped up Pete Kott, Vic Kohring, and Bruce Weyhrauch, delivering all three handcuffed men through the front door of the Juneau Federal Building where staff, cruise ship tourists, and the press lined office windows pointing, yelling, and motioning others to the historic scene. A twenty seven page indictment accused all three of soliciting favors from VECO Bill Allen and Rick Smith in exchange for votes on the PPT during the 2006 regular Legislative session, as well as the two special sessions that followed.

Kott and Weyhrauch were arraigned on multiple charges of bribery, extortion, wire and mail fraud; Kohring was charged with extortion and bribery. Each pleaded "not guilty" and each was released to await trial. The charging documents also referred to a former "Senator A" who worked in concert with the group, but who was not indicted. The press speculated that "Senator A" was likely Senator Ben Stevens, who had resigned only months before. John Wolfe, Stevens' Seattle lawyer, said Stevens didn't know who "Senator A" was and maintained "Stevens is innocent of any and all criminal activity."

After months of anticipation, the shoe had finally dropped. But it really didn't hit the floor until three days later when the Department of Justice announced, *Bill J. Allen, CEO and part owner of VECO Corporation, and Richard L. Smith, VECO Vice President have pleaded guilty to providing more than $400,000 in corrupt payments to public officials from the State of Alaska. Allen and Smith each pleaded guilty at hearings in federal court today in Anchorage, Alaska, to a three count information charging them with bribery, conspiracy to commit bribery, extortion, mail and wire fraud and conspiracy to defraud the Internal Revenue Service.*

Dressed in a gray suit, white shirt, red tie, and black cowboy boots, Allen stood in court and in his characteristic slow, gravelly drawl, admitted to conspiring with five current and former members of the Alaska legislature. He also acknowledged that he cooperated in the federal corruption investigation in exchange for immunity from prosecution for his son and daughter and special consideration at sentencing. In charging documents the government stated that more than half of the money went to former senator Ben Stevens for phony consulting fees.

Reached by phone in Seattle, Attorney Wolfe said again, "Mr. Stevens is surprised to learn that Bill Allen has pled guilty to various federal crimes and hopes that Mr. Allen is not falsely accusing former and current members of the Alaska legislature in order to mitigate his admitted criminality." The charging documents also identified an unindicted *Senator B*, who Allen later identified as Senator John Cowdery, of sinking-vessel fame.

As it turned out, Smith and Allen started cooperating with the FBI in August 2006, a couple of days after Senator Dyson introduced Allen to Agent Kepner who, as we know, can be very persuasive.

———•———

By June 2007 Kepner and the *Corrupt Bastard Catchers* had signed up enough *Corrupt Bastard Club* players to field a baseball team, with five in the dugout and an active recruitment strategy to beef up the squad with two nationally recognized heavy-hitting free agents. The *Corrupt Bastard Club* starting nine were Tom Anderson, Pete Kott, Vic Kohring, Bruce Weyhrauch, Bill Bobrick, Bill Allen, Rick Smith, Ben Stevens, and John Cowdery. Entrepreneur Bill Weimar, former Alaska senator Jerry Ward, former Alaska representative Beverly Masek and some other VECO executives warmed the bench. Club agents were also aggressively recruiting U.S. senator Ted Stevens, U.S. congressman Don Young, former Murkowski chief of staff Jim Clark and local millionaire fur trader and world-class poker aficionado Perry Green

Now, there's nothing really orthodox about Perry Green except his faith, which if measured by business success and personal wealth must have met YHWH's approval (or grace to look the other way). The son of a pioneer Anchorage fur trader, Green spins a colorful and charismatic presence in Alaska sociopolitical circles, particularly when the conversation turns to gambling. Perry has won three World Series of Poker bracelets and amassed an impressive eight hundred thousand dollars in live tournament winnings. Committed to diversifying Alaska's oil dependent economy, Green evidently convinced Pete Kott to sponsor HB 272, a bill legalizing card rooms in any Alaska community wanting to pass an ordinance authorizing the games. The bill passed the House in May 2005 and died in the Senate during the 2006 session, but not without attracting the *Corrupt Bastard Catchers* attention. The FBI suspected that *Green Backs* and *greenbacks* were the catalytic combination that sailed the bill through the House and on to the Senate.

After the toss, the *Corrupt Bastard Catchers* took to the field and the *Corrupt Bastards Club* starting batter, Tom Anderson, stepped up to the plate. The opening game of the series was played at the United States District Court in Anchorage under a late June midnight sun. Anderson hired local defense attorney Paul Stoeckler, a reported legend in his own mind among the Alaska Bar. In stark contrast to his strutting *Boston Legal* mentors, Stoeckler unveiled a disarmingly simple defense strategy: Anderson was just a nice, naïve guy going out of his way to help others when he was entrapped by two wily, seasoned political operatives who, in trouble themselves, testified against Anderson to save their necks. That would be Bill Bobrick, who did, and I, who didn't. But why screw up a good defense with small things like the truth.

The government's case was equally simple: Anderson was a debt-ridden politician who sold his office for cash and favors. And as evidence, the government played three days of devastating secret audio and visual recordings of Anderson soliciting and accepting money (*from* me) in exchange for official acts (*for* me). The trial lasted over a week and went to the jury on a Friday.

On Monday, July 9, 2007 Agent Kepner was told the jury would announce its verdict after the lunch recess. This was the first case to go to trial and she (like everyone else) was on pins and needles. At 1:30 p.m. U.S. District Court Judge James Sedwick asked the jury foreman if he had a verdict.

The foreman said, "We do, your Honor. We find the defendant, Thomas T. Anderson, guilty on all seven counts of criminal conspiracy to corrupt the public process."

Standing side by side, Anderson and Stoeckler both appeared stunned by the verdict. Anderson sighed and hung his head as all seven guilty findings were announced, one by one. After the jury left the room, a weary Anderson told reporters, "I'm devastated. The prosecution has criminalized being a legislator over this past year, and I think I fell victim to that. *Guilt by association*, words Anderson would later regret.

Kepner took a deep breath, exhaled, leaned toward U.S. Attorney Bottini and whispered, "Next batter."

A few months later Anderson stood before sentencing judge Sedwick and admitted he broke the law, violated the public trust, and must be punished. He said he hadn't understood the real significance of his acts until trial, when he saw the undercover videos of him scheming with the lobbyist and consultant. "I was embarrassed, I don't know how much more wrong that could have been." A humbled Stoeckler agreed with his client, admitting that he just didn't understand how they had missed the significance of the government's evidence. Kepner and Bottini wondered the same thing, but chalked it up to *Lethal* McGuire's sirenic charms.

At sentencing a sober Judge Sedwick looked up at the packed courtroom and said, "Mr. Anderson sold the public trust. He took the money because he wanted the money. We cannot tolerate the kind of behavior in which he engaged." He then sentenced Anderson to five years in federal prison with five years probation. Anderson was booked into the federal penitentiary at rainy Sheridan, Oregon on December 3, 2007, only six days after his cooperating coconspirator, Bill Bobrick, was sentenced to a mere *five months* in prison and *five month's* home confinement for his lead role in the very same offenses.

One of the factors in Bobrick's favor was taking immediate responsibility for his crimes. Another was his continued cooperation after receiving a certain New Year's day telephone call from Alaska Senator Lesil McGuire. But Republicans chalked it up to the historical dispensation of reciprocal grace and mercy shown to Alaska's small, but privileged family of Democrats, of which Bobrick was former Chair and Judge Sedwick and wife high-profile members.

Local TV news interviewed Anderson the evening before his scheduled departure to prison. Kepner was at home and happened to catch the brief interview. She turned and commented, "It's gonna take Tom a while to figure out just how *lethal* McGuire's help was." Watching Anderson, Kepner's husband replied, "Well, he has a long time to figure it out." (A month later Bill Bobrick slipped quietly out of town and checked into a private, minimum-security campus in sun-soaked southern California operated by Management and Training Corporation [MTC] under contract with the Federal Bureau of Prisons. Not a bad gig. Guess it pays to *cooperate.*)

July 2007 wasn't just a tough month for low-hanging fruit. It proved a particularly difficult month for the entire Alaska congressional delegation. One week after the Anderson conviction, U.S. Senator Lisa Murkowski made headlines after a friend gave her a good deal on an acre of land she intended to use as a family retreat from the harsh demands of life in the nation's capital. Unfortunately, the friend was influential land developer Bob Penney, who "in appreciation for all he's done for Alaska and the country," turned a modest fifteen thousand dollar personal investment by U.S. Senator Ted Stevens into an eyebrow-raising one hundred thirty five thousand dollar gain at the same time Stevens was putting four and a half million dollars of Federal Earmarks into Penney's Kenai River Sport-fishing Association.

KRSA hosts the annual Kenai King Salmon Fishing Classic fundraiser for Ted Stevens and Lisa Murkowski who then invite other influential members of Congress and well- heeled guests for a good time on the river. Every summer, without *Delay*, privileged guests cast their *Lott* to *Duke* it out on *Craig's* list of salmon-slammin' anglers, far *Inouye* the best event of the summer, unless you count Don Young's *Cunning ham* pork roast (sorry, I couldn't help myself). By the way, these are the same Stevens and Penney who partnered up with VECO Bill Allen in *So Long Birdie*, a retired racehorse who hooks up with young fillies for pictures and a price.

To complicate matters further, Murkowski's land was prime Kenai riverfront property right next door to Penney, reportedly purchased for $100,000 below fair market value and sweetheart-financed by a bank in a small Alaska town eight hundred miles south (of which Lisa Murkowski is a former director and her sister a shareholder and current director). Not recognizing the one hundred thousand dollar windfall as a reportable gift, nor wanting the property *to become a distraction from the major challenges facing Alaska*, a week later Senator Murkowski announced that she was selling the property back to Penney. A chagrined Murkowski said, "I guess I've always known that I live in a glass house as a public figure, but I guess I'm not going to be living in a glass house on the Kenai River."

The month of July was also no cakewalk for *Congressman for all Alaska,* Don Young. In the July campaign disclosure reports for third-quarter spending, *Alaskans for Don Young* reported that between March 10, 2007 and June 15, 2007 the campaign spent over two hundred forty thousand dollars retaining the services of Akin Gump Strauss & Hauser, a premier Washington DC law firm that handles, among other areas, white-collar criminal defense. There was a lot of press speculation that the extraordinary disclosure related to *quid pro quo* campaign contributions from a Milwaukee businessman who benefited from new truck-hauling regulations that Young pushed through in 2005 as a part of a major transportation spending bill. Others believed it was the ten million dollar Coconut Road project that helped out Florida real estate developer Daniel Aronoff only days after Aronoff helped raise forty thousand dollars for Young's re-election. And while those projects, and more, would eventually come under grand jury scrutiny, Congressman Young knew exactly what it was all about. He just wasn't saying. You know, "on advice of counsel," a well worn phrase over the next year.

—————

It was early evening as Kepner slowly turned down the maple-lined street of vintage suburban DC houses. Ignoring the GPS she glanced at a photograph, looked to her left and said, "Here it is." She pulled into the driveway in front of a two-car garage, stopped, and shut down the engine as Chad quietly stepped out onto the concrete and felt for his weapon. A floodlight suddenly illuminated the driveway and Chad backed into a shadow. Like in a stage play, the large garage door slowly lifted, revealing a pair of scraggly, paint-stained tennis shoes, baggy sweats, rotund belly, folded arms, white Colonel Sanders beard, and frowning countenance of the *Congressman for all Alaska*. Kepner stepped out of the car and said, "Congressman Young, my name is Mary Beth Kepner. This is my partner, Chad Joy. We're with the FBI and we'd like to ask you a few questions."

Young irritably said, "I have a scheduling secretary, an office, and office hours. Feel free to make an appointment. Just who'n the hyell do you think you are?"

Kepner replied, "I'm very sorry Congressman Young. We'd be happy to make an appointment, or drop by during your office hours. We just thought you'd prefer to talk to us in a less public place." Turning, she said, "Chad, let's go."

Young thought for a moment and said, "Wait, wait, you know, I get hounded by people all day long and, well crap, you know. Come on in. What's on yer mind?"

Kepner smiled and followed Young into the kitchen where they all pulled up chairs around an average, middle-class-looking table surrounded by things most people have in their kitchens, such as empty pizza boxes, beer cans, cigar butts, an open box of licorice twists, and a pile of dirty dishes.

Kepner sat down, opened a file and spread a bunch of pictures out on the table. "Do you recognize these?" she said.

Young picked them up, and after a bit, said, "Sure, that's the golf tournament VECO throws every year to help keep me in touch with my constituents."

"How 'bout this one," Kepner said as she slid the picture across the table. Young looked down, paused, looked up with a stone face and said, "What do you want?"

Kepner replied, "We want to talk to you about Bill Allen, Rick Smith, pig roasts, golf tournaments, earmarks, campaign contributions, and your IRS returns."

Young said he'd need to talk to an attorney and Kepner replied, "No hurry, but that would be a very wise contact, Mr. Congressman. Let's stay in touch." Kepner and Joy stood, thanked Congressman Young for his hospitality and said they could see their way to the door.

As they backed out of the drive Chad said, "So, how'd I do?"

Kepner replied, "Oh you were too tres' scary."

"No, really, how'd I do?" Chad persisted.

Kepner said, "Just perfect. He knows we're serious. What's your bet on who he's calling right now?"

———

By the first quarter of 2008 Alaskans for Don Young reported tapping Young's campaign contribution war chest a staggering $1.2 million in legal defense fees. Over a million dollars went to Akin, Gump, Strauss & Hauser, and a curious twenty thousand dollars was paid to former Alaska senator Ben Stevens' Seattle criminal defense attorney John Wolfe. With no end in sight and defense fees averaging over seventy thousand dollars per month, Young finally requested and received approval from the House Ethics Committee to set up a separate defense fund. Concerned over hemorrhaging campaign contributions, Young spokesman Mike Anderson explained, "We had some feedback from some folks who said they wanted to help us out, but they wanted to do so through a legal defense fund, so we went ahead and did that in the hopes that our campaign funds can be freed up." This enabled Young's contributors to donate five thousand dollars per year to his defense fund above the maximum annual campaign contribution limit of four thousand six hundred dollars for primary and general elections.

The discovery of Congressman Young's extraordinary new alliance with American Trial Lawyers (a group he historically spurned) wasn't the end of his 2007 summer of pain. In the past, VECO Bill Allen had hosted Young's annual Pig Roast fundraiser at Allen's Bootlegger Cove home. For years checkbook-laden guests had filed past a grinning and greeting, apron draped Don Young standing next to a huge barbecue. Stuffed into the barbecue, snout-to-hoof, was an enormous hog, garnished with a tasteful VECO logo. Since Bill Allen was detained, or otherwise occupied with federal business, former Alaska governor Bill Sheffield agreed to host the prestigious 2007 event at his Cook Inlet bluff home in Anchorage.

Bill Sheffield's sprawling new contemporary home abuts Earthquake Park, the historic site of an affluent community of seventy five homes which slid into thirty foot crevasses or floated out to sea during the 1964 Good Friday earthquake. At 9.2 on the Richter Scale, the historic shaker is the most powerful North American earthquake of record. A bit of a historic shaker and mover in his own right, Sheffield was evidently willing to play the odds that the big quake was a once-per-lifetime event. I imagine there's some basis for his optimism, since he's landed on his feet after more than one minor quake in his life, impeachment being among the most noteworthy.

During the mid '80s former governor Sheffield tried to steer a multimillion dollar government lease to a major campaign contributor. A grand jury investigated, found him unfit to hold office and recommended impeachment. By a two-thirds vote the legislature agreed to hold hearings, but with improbable memory lapses and a high-profile Watergate defense attorney, Sheffield narrowly averted becoming the first U.S. governor to be impeached since the 1930s (but again, that's another story). About half of the seventy demonstrators who lined up outside Sheffield's $1,000-per-plate (*suggested contribution*) pig roast were too young to remember the Sheffield scandal, but not the escapades of Congressman for all Alaska (except the protestors) Don Young.

Like any good tailgate party, the rowdy demonstrators sat in lawn chairs and leaned against trucks and cars drinking beer, eating snacks, shouting "oink, oink" at guests, and waving signs opposed to campaign contributions, consulting contracts, conservatives, corruption, crooks, cranks, and cronies. Inside, an illustrious crowd of lobbyists, executives, foundation directors, legislators, Republican Party officials and talk radio hosts dined on beer, bottled water, and roast pig, as Stevens, Murkowski, and an apronless Don Young moved quickly through the crowd, out the back door and into idling decoy vehicles while combative verbal fire diverted the protesters.

A week later Alaskans for Don Young hosted a picnic on the Park Strip in downtown Anchorage, passing out Mountain Dew and Diet Pepsi as hundreds of people stood in line for a plate of free food and a glimpse of Young manning the dog and burger grill. A few feet away from the grill a handful of protesters periodically chanted, *FBI, FBI* and Young would look up from the grill, grin, flail his spatula, pump his arms, wag his hips and boogie down singing, *they'll never get the best of me.* Through a break in the crowd, Chad could just make out the VECO logo garnishing Young's big black mobile barbecue and wondered if Young had a matching body tattoo on his big white wagging arse.

The first indication that *they* might indeed be getting the best of him came a few months later, when the barn-storming campaign contribution magnet attracted a meager forty thousand dollars in final quarter contributions, ten thousand dollars less than his little-known, overly ambitious, Democratic challenger had collected during the same quarter. Two weeks later Washington Post conservative commentator George Will enshrined Don Young as the national poster child for Congressional misfeasance, noting, "Coconut Road near Fort Meyers looks like any other concrete ribbon near housing developments, golf courses and shopping malls in this state's booming southwest. But like another fragrant slab of recent pork, the $223 million "Bridge To Nowhere" in Alaska, Coconut Road leads to somewhere darkly fascinating. It runs straight into Washington's earmark culture of waste, corruption and anti-constitutional deviousness."

Will said the Coconut Road earmark was "smudged with the fingerprints of Alaska's Republican Rep. Don Young...the subject of an FBI investigation concerning another matter (facing) strong opposition to a 19th term." Months later, over the objection of Alaska Senators Ted Stevens and Lisa Murkowski, the U.S. Senate voted 64 to 28 to ask the Justice Department to investigate Young's Coconut Road earmark. In a tribute to *The Godfather,* this *Don's* organization was also unraveling and rival families were circling for the kill.

———

Anchorage Daily News
August 8, 2007

Ben Stevens, the former state senator who has come under scrutiny along with his father in a broad federal public corruption probe has taken a new job far from his Anchorage home. The younger Stevens has been hired as a crewman aboard a work boat supporting Dutch oil giant Shell's planned Arctic Ocean exploratory drilling campaign.

The job marks a return to a former seafaring life for Stevens, who for many years ran crab fishing boats in the Bering Sea. A Shell contractor, Bering Marine Corp hired Stevens as mate and relief skipper aboard the 121 foot combo tug and landing craft Arctic Seal. Bering Marine President Rick gray said, "We're real proud to have Ben working for us." Ben Stevens, who is living aboard the boat, could not be reached.

By the end of July 2007, senior U.S. Senator Ted Stevens would probably have gladly traded jobs with his son. For a solid month the Washington Post, Associated Press, Yahoo, New York Times, Congressional Quarterly, Roll Call, and CNN pounded out major stories on the senior senator, ranging from questionable use of Congressional earmarks to a rumored federal grand jury criminal investigation. But the grand finale occurred when federal agents raided Stevens' Alaska home in Girdwood.

Girdwood is thirty seven miles south of Anchorage. Tightly tucked into a box canyon of the Chugach Mountains, Girdwood looks a lot like a Swiss Alps village would look if the urban planners had been miners, hippies, and ski bums. In the early 1900s, an Irishman named

Joe Girdwood staked four gold claims on Crow Creek and set up a supply shack for gold prospectors trying to squeeze a living out of the frigid mountain drainage. The government shut down the mining operations during World War II and Girdwood limped along as a place to stop on the road and rail passage to Southcentral Alaska's main open water seaport at Seward.

In 1964 the same earthquake that rocked the landscape under Don Young's Pork Roast fundraiser sank the town of Girdwood ten feet, leaving the community several feet lower than the surging daily tide of Cook Inlet. The community moved up-canyon, providing infrastructure for the fledgling Alyeska Ski Lodge, and evolved into a charming little granola-crunching service community. Today, Girdwood offers world-class skiing, hiking, rafting, Cajun cuisine, and the famous Girdwood Forest Fair, where locals sell handicrafts reminiscent of the Berkeley / Haight-Ashbury '60s hippie movement, smoke a little dope, kiss trees, and talk about the old days.

Girdwood's laid-back alpine serenity was shattered the morning of July 30, 2007, as wide-eyed neighbors watched six federal cars and a satellite truck park in front of Stevens' Girdwood residence and a dozen more roll into the Alyeska ski resort day lodge parking lot. As neighbors stared, a locksmith picked open the door. Throughout the afternoon agents came and went, hauling off loads of undisclosed personal property, taking pictures, itemizing fixtures, and scaling the steep chalet metal roof. Friend or foe, awestruck bystanders and reporters winced in wonder at the muscular Federal intrusion into the property rights of the senior U.S. senator of our free constitutional republic. Neither the senator, nor his family or friends were at the scene, but in a brief press conference the following day, Brendan Sullivan (of Oliver North Iran Contra fame) acknowledged that he had been retained by Senator Stevens and had a "long-standing practice not to comment on such matters."

Chapter Six
Ted and Don's Grand Adventure

He waited off stage as the confused cascade of random notes merged into a warm, harmonious crescendo of symphonic bliss. On cue, the naked baritone smiled, stepped through the curtain and pierced the morning calm crooning…

Earmarks in the niight, exchanging glances
Wondering in the niight
What were the chances we'd be shaking hannds
Before the lobbyin' was throuugh
Something in the dealll was so inviting
Something in your smile was so igniting
Something in my mind
Told me I must do youu
Strangers in the niight, two greedy people
We were strannngers in the niight
Up to that moment
When we said our first hello
Little did we knoww
The deal was just a glance away
One Earmark and we dance awayyyy
AND ever since that niiight we've slept togetherr
Brothers at first siight, corrupt and cleverrr
Offshore trust deliight
For stranngerrs innn the niiiight.

"Honey, it's the phone, and enough with the song, you're gonna strain something!" I turned off the shower, stepped into the steaming room, looked at the caller ID, picked up the phone and yelled, "Kepner, for crying out loud, it's seven a.m.!"

A voice on the other end replied, "I don't know what *your* problem is, I started two hours ago, right after I finished working out."

I said, "Right, you're so full of it, what do you want anyway?"

Kepner said, "We're having a little bio briefing on Ted and Don. It's nothing super secure, but someone thought there could be information or something that might trigger a thought, or recollection, in your twisted little selectively forgetful mind. You wanna come down?"

"Sure, what time?" I said.

Kepner replied, "We'll wait for you. The coffee's on."

———

Ad. 2008. Senator Theodore Fulton Stevens and Congressman Donald Edwin Young are making history as the oldest and, perhaps, most successful Congressional Earmark tag-team wrestlers in U.S. history. With Young's trademark uplifted middle finger and Stevens' Hulk tie and temperament, year after year Alaska's hot-tempered and feisty duo leap from the ropes of congressional seniority kicking, gouging, and body-slamming their fair and disproportionate share of the federal discretionary spending pork pie.

While a political term of art, *earmarks* are easy to understand. Every year the executive branch (President) submits a spending plan (budget) to both bodies (Senate & House) of Congress. Each body then assigns sections of the proposed budget to various committees who analyze and ultimately adjust the numbers to reflect the majority's spending priorities. When the Senate and House each pass their own world view of how the executive branch should spend the money, a select group from each body meets in "conference" to arm-wrestle a compromise intended to satisfy the spending priorities of the President, Senate, and House.

"Earmarks" are monies that were not requested by the President, but added to the budget after the public process by individual members of Congress. Like stealth missiles, many earmarks slip in under the radar with no debate, vote, or knowledge by the general membership through the Conference Committee process, long after votes on spending have been cast. A rankled President Bush recently commented,

"...over 90% of earmarks never make it to the floor of the House and Senate...you didn't vote them into law and I didn't sign them into law. Yet they're treated as if they have the force of law." Over the past twenty years, *earmarking* has grown from Congressional anomaly to accepted practice, and represents nearly thirty billion dollars in discretionary annual spending.

Many earmarks have little to do with fire, life, safety, and other basic but necessary services. These concerns are ordinarily covered by the capital and operating budgets for all to see. Earmarks are usually dedicated to the parochial in-state projects, services, studies, groups, causes, and special interests of those privileged enough to have, or acquire, access to senior members of Congress. Those who have direct access, of course, are family, friends, current and prior staff and their respective networks of affiliation. But if one doesn't have the good fortune of being connected to privilege, the same benefits can be acquired through campaign contributions and other favors. Not necessarily a *quid pro quo*, of course, it just takes a lot of money to win and retain a seat in Congress, or any other legislative body.

So when red-carpet contributors and insiders have problems, or great ideas, lawmakers lend an *ear* and *mark* the request. It's really not surprising then that *Earmarkees* are usually, well, the friends, family, affiliates, and supporters of *Earmarkers*. It just kinda works out that way. Again, not always a *quid pro quo*, but it's sure easy to see how the practice can slip into a bit of tit-for-tat primate lice pickin' and back scratchin.' Take, for example, Ted and Don, Alaska's *go-to guys* for federal largesse and favors.

Ted Stevens was appointed to the U.S. Senate in 1968 after incumbent Bob Bartlett succumbed to heart failure. A decorated World War II veteran, Stevens graduated from Harvard Law School, set his sights on politics and never looked back. For thirty years Stevens represented Alaska without a hint of tarnish on his reputation. Working his way up the Club ladder, Stevens gained a reputation as a scrappy and savvy defender and apologist for Alaska and Alaskans. By 2007 he was the longest serving Republican in the Senate and had served as President Pro Tempore, chairman and ranking member of Defense Appropriations, and chairman and ranking member of Senate Appropriations, which approves every dollar of federal discretionary spending.

According to a breaking story in the *Los Angeles Times*, the senior

Stevens really didn't come under much scrutiny until 1997 when, after years of delivering for Alaska, he decided it was time to build up the ol' retirement portfolio and asked his brother-in-law, Bill Bittner, for a hand. Bittner, a friend and neighbor of VECO Bill Allen, contacted a business partner and particularly savvy attorney-turned-developer named John Rubini, who said he would be honored to help the senator. Rubini arranged for Stevens to put up fifty thousand dollars as interest in a new syndicate called JLS Properties. Rubini and two other partners personally guaranteed the debts of the partnership and agreed, if necessary, to capitalize the venture. The group bought and sold a succession of properties and, within three years, Stevens' equity climbed from fifty to two hundred fifty thousand dollars. Not a bad tip for a relative.

About the same time, Rubini and Bittner bid on a four hundred fifty million dollar contract to privatize the Elmendorf Air Force Base housing (a federal installation bordering the Municipality of Anchorage). The Air Force declined their proposal because the investment group "lacked capacity and adequate financing." Rubini went to Stevens who, as Chairman of Appropriations, enlisted Kenai Fishing Classic buddy and Military Construction Subcommittee Chair Conrad Burns to write a letter to the Secretary of the Air Force threatening to cut the privatization moneys for failure to award the contract to Rubini's group. A similar letter from the corresponding House sub-committee was arranged and, voila, the Air Force folded.

One can only hope international terrorists and hostile nations never really figure out how to pull the political strings on our national energy spending. I can hear it now, *Mr Secretary, Iran was the lowest bidder and possesses the latest technology to jump-start our atrophied domestic nuclear energy need.* But Stevens waived off critics saying he was, "just looking out for an Alaskan company that was getting short shrift from the Department of Defense."

Like a cause-and-effect succession of natural events (i.e., tipping the first in a long line of dominoes), Stevens' successful intervention triggered another Rubini decision to include Stevens and JLS Properties in an investment that would finally unlock the door to the Senate Millionaires Club to which he aspired. Again, the senior Senator didn't have to agree to guarantee or capitalize like the other partners, he simply allowed his earlier "equity position" to be used to secure financing for the new project, an awe inspiring thirty five million dollar structure that now houses the corporate offices of Arctic Slope Region Corporation under an annual six million dollar twenty year lease. Arctic Slope Region Inc. is a one billion dollar per year enterprise, the very existence of which is due, in large part, to the support of Alaska Senator Ted Stevens, their new landlord.

By 2006, earmarks, appropriations, regulatory revisions, enabling legislation, gifts, and partnerships benefiting Stevens, his son, friends, business associates, and affiliates triggered another *perfect storm* of curiosity over a small appropriation to the little-known Seward SeaLife Center, a popular federally subsidized tourist attraction and research center in the city of Seward, south of Anchorage on the Kenai Peninsula. The appropriation enabled one of Stevens' former congressional aides (and son Ben's business partner), Trevor McCabe, to sell a conspicuously timed acquisition to the National Park Service for land needed to build a new twenty million dollar visitor center.

The city of Seward was to receive and manage the federally earmarked acquisition funds, but the negotiations over McCabe's property hit a major snag, the asking price. A month later Stevens used his power over federal appropriations to transfer the one million six hundred thousand dollars remaining in the National Park Service *property acquisition fund* to the Seward SeaLife Center to help the facility and revitalize downtown Seward. The SeaLife Center then spent more than five hundred fifty thousand dollars of the federal windfall to buy McCabe's property. Within months Federal subpoenas were popping up among Stevens' family, friends, and affiliates like dandelions on a golf course, culminating in a search warrant linking the senior Stevens' Girdwood house to a gratuitous expansion by good friend and fishing buddy VECO Bill Allen. Needless to say, Senator Stevens and associates have had better years.

Not to be outdone, by 2007 Congressman Young was receiving his own share of scrutiny for similar past and current practices. From 2001 to 2005, as chairman of House Transportation, Young collected six and a half million dollars in "campaign contributions" from people who neither live nor vote in Alaska. Donations that can, evidently, even be used to hire the best criminal defense team money can buy.

Among the Congressman's pet projects were two five million dollar allotments benefiting a Syracuse, New York, shopping mall developer who (with a little help from family, employees and "friends") donated over thirty three thousand dollars in campaign contributions; a one hundred million dollar appropriation to add four *truck lanes* to a three hundred fifty mile length of Interstate 81, for which appreciative executives, family and friends made more than two hundred thirty five thousand dollars in campaign contributions; a four hundred thirty two million dollar appropriation for five central California highway projects, for which thankful benefactors donated thirty four thousand dollars at just one San Jose fundraiser; and a seventy two million dollar link between Pine Bluff, Arkansas and a projected future Interstate 69 which netted Young a cool two hundred seven thousand dollars in 2004 and 2005.

While the totals are hard to trace and calculate, in November 2007 the *Anchorage Daily News* reported that just seven randomly selected earmark appropriations totaling two hundred fifty five million dollars netted Young five hundred seventy five thousand dollars in campaign donations for projects that had nothing to do with Alaska, an observation that didn't escape the politically insightful eyes of Alaska's new Governor, Sarah Palin.

But the earmarks that received the most attention were the now infamous "Bridges To Nowhere." The earmarks were a tag-team effort to appropriate more than four hundred million dollars to jumpstart construction of a bridge connecting the city of Ketchikan to an island hosting its municipal airport, and a two-mile bridge across Cook Inlet's Knik Arm connecting Anchorage to undeveloped land on the other side. Federal support for state transportation infrastructure is an appropriate use of federal funds. And who better to determine state infrastructure needs than the residents of the state and their congressional delegation? In spite of the national bad rap, the projects make sense even if they aren't everyone's top priority. The devil wasn't in the *what*, it was in the *how* of the appropriations.

Young and Stevens agreed to support the two projects in 2002, after Governor Murkowski established a Knik bridge planning authority (KABATA) and expressed a similar vision for the Ketchikan/Gravina Island bridge. Young began substantive planning for the earmarks in 2003 while he was House Transportation and Infrastructure chairman. The earmarks were scheduled to appear in the 2005 federal budget. Between 2002 and 2004 the real estate on the far side of the proposed

Knik Arm crossing became an inside traders' dream, as Senator Stevens' chief of staff, George Lowe, former top aide Lisa Sutherland, former aide Trevor McCabe, and Don Young's son-in-law, Art Nelson, individually and through a newly incorporated Point Bluff LLC (with more inside traders), purchased seventy acres of strategically situated land. They knew, of course, that no bridges were possible without federal funding, but unlike the general public, they controlled, or had access to the inside information needed to mitigate the risk of land speculation. In the end the bridges didn't collapse from failure in design, they crumbled from the perception of a corrupt foundation. *KABATA* is now seeking private investors while the privileged speculator properties have doubled in value.

Under re-election pressure and growing distrust, months later Alaska's congressional delegation held a press conference and promised a new day of "sunlight and transparency," saying they would begin disclosing every request from the state for specially earmarked federal money. Stevens looked around at the room full of reporters and said, "The whole idea is to try and have people understand, those who want to ask us for money, have them understand how many other people are asking and to really have people here understand that we're not dreaming these up." Borrowing a line from the Bill Clinton campaign, no one noticed the elephant in the room shouting, *"It's not the earmarks, it's the insider trading, stupid!"*

Anchorage Daily News
By Sean Cockerham
December 10, 2007

The Palin Administration, citing a need to improve the State's credibility, plans to ask Alaska's congressional delegation for far fewer earmarks in the coming year…Karen Rehfeld, Palin's budget chief said the state has to be sensitive to a national perception that Alaska has a lot of money and shouldn't always be asking for so much from the federal treasury…A favorite target is the so-called "bridges to nowhere" for Ketchikan and the Knik Arm inserted by Alaska Representative Don Young into the five-year transportation bill in 2005…Palin says Alaska

needs to change its national image, change that includes trying
to become less dependent on the federal government.

One clairvoyant Palin month later, in his State of the Union address,
President Bush vowed to veto any future spending bills crossing his
desk that did not cut the number and cost of earmarks in half. He said,
"The people's trust in their government is undermined by congressional earmarks, special interest projects that are often snuck in at the
last minute, without discussion or debate." After the speech a belliger-
ent Ted Stevens shrugged his shoulders and dismissed the President's
concern as just another skirmish in the never-ending battle between
Congress and the President over federal spending. Stevens quipped,
"When I put in money to put a bridge in a national park I don't ask
for the money, I just take that money from somewhere else in the national park budget...if the committee agrees with me we take out the
President's priority and put in mine (of course Stevens is usually chair,
co-chair, or senior member of the committee).
Listening to the President's and Stevens' remarks, a concerned fellow Republican (U.S. Senator Tom Coburn of Oklahoma) disagreed
with both, saying, "The American people want to see the Washington earmark factory shut down, not downsized...How many more
earmarks related investigations, search warrants and indictments have
to be issued before Congress gets the message that it's time to end
this practice." I gave Coburn an affirming off-stage nod, turned off my
computer, and thought about the problem of earmarks as the distant
cascade of random notes merged into a warm, inviting crescendo of
symphonic bliss. On cue, I stepped through the curtain, smiled into
the showering applause and crooned the final score to *Ted And Don's
Grand Adventure*:

> Earmarks in the niiight, exchanging glances,
> wondering in the niiight
> what were the chances they'd be sharing cells
> before the year was throuugh
> Something in the dealll was so indicting
> something in their smile was so exciting,
> something in my mind
> told me they're prob'ly screwwwed

Sturrrrangers in the niight, two pompous asses,
they were sturrrrangers in the niight
up to the moment
when they said their first 'Hell No',
little did we know
their deals were just a glance away,
search warrants and we danced all day, 'CAUUSSE
ever since that niiight they've worked together
brethren at first siiiight, corrupt and cleverrr
offshore trust delight
it's FBI toniiiightttt…it's F-B-IIII, tooniiight.

Good night L'il Darl'n.

Chapter Seven
Three-For-Three and Me

The second batter in the *Corrupt Bastards Club* lineup was former Alaska House Speaker Pete Kott. Pete graduated from high school in 1967 and spent twenty two years in the Air Force, retiring at age forty with the rank of captain. Three years later Pete won a seat in the Alaska House and served several unremarkable years trying to find a niche in a bigger game. Opportunity knocked when Bill Allen noticed Pete's good ol' boy charm. Allen saw leadership potential and after years of corporate management, he recognized that Pete's hunger for the *good life* and his *fall-on-a-sword* personality would serve them both well, a little too well, as it turned out.

In opening statements, Federal Prosecutor Nicholas Marsh told jurors that Kott abused the public trust by using his legislative office for personal financial gain. "Pete Kott wanted money and a job and crossed the line…his own words will be used against him." With the outstretched arms of a revival altar-call, Marsh implored, "You will hear him say he *sooold* his *soouul* to the devil!"

Kott's attorney, Jim Wendt, dismissed Marsh's accusations as misconstrued and overblown. He said Kott didn't receive any personal benefit from anything he did on Allen's behalf and urged, "There's nothing illegal about working with lobbyists or others [I imagine that includes the devil] for the same end…if he is guilty of anything, he's guilty of working to get a pipeline."

Battle lines drawn, the prosecution started calling witnesses. First on deck was FBI Special Agent Steve Dunphy, who had recorded and monitored the action in Suite 604. From Cincinnati, Dunphy was one of a growing army of volunteer federal agents and technicians responding to Kepner's appeal for help in the rapidly escalating case. For an entire afternoon Dunphy laid out the authority, dates, time, places, techniques, subjects, and highlights of recorded and photographed conversations and meetings.

The next day jurors were treated to hour after hour of Suite 604 video and audio recordings of conversations and phone calls. Many visibly winced as Kott and the Suite 604 regulars smoked, drank, belched, laughed, swore, and exchanged crude familiarities and coarse gestures. Like scenes from a second-rate movie jurors sat mesmerized by *quid pro quo* schemes, threats, cash, and promises favoring the mutual special interests of Big Oil, Bill Allen, and Pete Kott. After a very long day, shell-shocked jurors and spectators quietly filed out the swinging doors of Courtroom B, stunned witnesses to a graphic and sickening gang rape of public trust.

On day three, a year after Senator Dyson introduced him to the FBI, a drawn and weary Bill Allen took the stand to a bi-partisan, standing-room-only crowd of past and current politicians, reporters, prosecutors, defense attorneys, and civics students. Unlike the swaggering Texan on the secret tapes, a haltering, visibly aged Allen testified all afternoon and well into the next day about dispensing job promises and cash, paying phony invoices and political polls, and conspiring with Kott to hold a twenty percent production tax rate that, in the testimony of one expert, was worth one hundred fifty million dollars per year to the Major Producers for every one percent increase above the twenty percent rate.

Allen had suffered a brain injury from a motorcycle accident a few years back that impaired his speech. At one point, while trying to explain the major producer's position on the PPT, a trembling and visibly frustrated Allen blurted out, "Wait, I gotta find this word." He bowed his head for what seemed an eternity in the packed courtroom, and finally proclaimed, *Certainty*! That's it, they wanted *certainty* that the taxes wouldn't be raised if they agreed to build a pipeline. He then recounted his phone call with ConocoPhillips president Jim Bowles, promising that Kott and Ben Stevens would see to it that the producers' fingerprints weren't on the push to hold the PPT tax at *20/20*.

The defense spent most of the fourth day trying to unravel Allen's testimony, but Allen wouldn't spin, fold, or mutilate his prior statements, maintaining that he "worked real hard try'n to make the truth and everythangg…to be fair." Allen said he agreed to cooperate with the government to save his grown children from indictments. "My family did get in the middle of this mess, so I'm gonna do what I told 'em [the government] I'm gonna do," replied Allen. Kott's attorney sneered out loud that Allen's motivation was really to get his sentence reduced. Allen replied, "You know, I really don't care. I've never asked them for a damn thing when it comes to my sentence. It'd be whatever happens. My life is about gone anyway."

Then, as if withheld for dramatic effect, Kott's attorney asked, "One of these allegations is that you helped Senator Ted Stevens with remodeling his house in Girdwood, isn't that true?"

Under oath Allen replied, "*yes*." An electrified courtroom gasped at both the revelation and implication. Reporters leaned into notepads and some left the room as Allen went on to describe VECO's two year investment in design, project management, labor, and material which doubled the size of U.S. Senator Ted Stevens' official Alaska residence. Seated stoically next to U.S. Attorney Marsh, only Kepner's closest associates recognized the Mona Lisa smile as another cat crawled out of the bag.

Allen was excused and former VECO Vice President Rick Smith was sworn in. Not to be outdone, Smith captivated the audience as he diverted his testimony from Pete Kott to other legislators involved in the network of conspiracy, bribery, and fraud. When asked to name the legislators he bribed, Smith replied, "That would be Vic Kohring, Pete Kott, Bruce Weyhrauch, Ben Stevens, and John Cowdery."

Smith went on to describe his role in organizing golf tournaments and pig roast fundraisers for U.S. Congressman Don Young with guest lists of two to four hundred names of reliable contributors. Smith said he hired the Marx Brothers, an upscale Anchorage restaurant, to cater the food and beverage, which ran $10,000 to $15,000 per event. When asked about Representative Tom Anderson's "sham" consulting contract with VECO, Smith agreed, smiled, and replied, "We never got any work out of it. I asked him to produce things for us. It didn't happen [for trial strategy reasons Anderson was never charged with this offense]." Smith wrapped up his testimony describing a special arrangement with a local bar, where he was able to launder money to provide non-reportable cash prizes at Don Young's golf tournaments.

On the ninth day of trial Pete Kott took the stand. As Kott was testifying, Governor Sarah Palin quietly slipped into the back row. She watched for a short while and, when asked about her appearance, later replied, "This is one of the most important series of trials in Alaska history." In the meantime, other than an apology for the graphic video displays of vulgar and crass behavior, Kott's self-serving testimony (admitting facts but denying culpability) revealed little and had even less impact on the jury. As one juror put it, "Kott said, 'I'll lie to my friends but I do have my principles.' How can you believe anything he says after that?"

After deliberating for a day, the jury convicted former Alaska Speaker of the House Pete Kott on three of four corruption charges, finding him guilty of bribery, extortion, and conspiracy and finding him not guilty of wire fraud. Asked her thoughts on the case, juror Susan Pollard summed up for every American the gravity of violations of public trust when she said, "I guess it was just more disturbing than it was significant. To see politics come to this shambles was so very disheartening."

When asked his opinion of the verdict, Senator Fred Dyson, who sat through most of the trial, said, "I expected it. I know all of the Kott family and my heart goes out to them. But I think the evidence was compelling. What these guys have done, not so much the money they took, but vandalizing the system and profoundly depreciating the public confidence in it, is so highly offensive."

Ten weeks later Pete Kott was sentenced to six years in Federal prison, three years probation and a $10,000 fine. Standing next to Prosecutor Marsh when the sentence was pronounced, Kepner looked over and said, "Next batter."

The third batter in the first inning of the *Corrupt Bastard Catchers vs Corrupt Bastards Club* was "straight talkin', sheet rockin', commie knockin', government sockin' Vic Kohring." Only a month after the Kott trial, the Kohring trial was in many respects quite similar. The prosecution argued that the case was about misuse of a position of public trust for personal financial gain. The defense portrayed Kohring as a victim who was broke and accepted cash as gifts from a well-heeled friend. The jury was, again, treated to hours of graphic footage showing Kohring accepting and stuffing wads of cash into his pockets from Bill Allen and then asking what he could do for Allen in return. In Kohring's case the graphic crudeness was the blatant *quid pro quo* of "gifts" for votes rather than the alcohol-driven bravado in the Kott tapes.

But the trial and results are best summarized by Juror #6, a blogger who, two days after the trial, wrote,

> Actually, Steve, there are no limits as to what I can or cannot discuss now that the trial is finished. Whew. It was hard to hold in all of my thoughts and emotions throughout the duration of the trial, so speaking about it now actually feels like 'venting.' In my opinion, there isn't a witch-hunt going on. I hate that the state and the feds are spending millions of dollars on this investigation, but the fact of the matter is it had to be done. There really are crooked politicians out there.
>
> In the eyes of the jury, Kohring was guilty based on two facts: Vic took money. And when Bill Allen told him that he was considering hauling Kohring out of Juneau two hours before the session was to end (which would have made him miss the final PPT vote) Kohring said, 'I'd have done it for ya, man.' And that was what swayed the jury. That one sentence. It showed us that Kohring was willing to disrupt his legislative duties for this guy…the same guy who had been slipping him cash. Those two things were what convinced us of his guilt.
>
> I remain
> Juror #6

Kohring was convicted and sentenced to three and a half years in prison for Conspiracy, Attempted Extortion and Bribery. He was found not guilty of Extortion. At sentencing Kohring told Judge Sedwick, "My conscience is clear…I refuse to cower before you in hopes of receiving a lighter sentence and know I'm risking retribution by standing my ground." Kepner listened as Kohring read his declaration of injustice and shook her head. He was the smallest fish in the pond and would probably have been sentenced to probation and a brief period of confinement, had he shown an ounce of contrition. The Corrupt Bastards Catchers were now 3 and 0 and heading for the big leagues.

On October 18, 2007 (the week of the Kohring trial), Governor Sarah Palin made good on her post regular session promise and called the Alaska Legislature back into special session to review the Petroleum Profits Tax (PPT) passed the year before. Palin maintained that the twenty two and a half percent tax rate did not deliver as much revenue as promised and the corruption probe tainted the product in the eyes of the public.

The Alaska Legislature is a sixty-member body and, throughout the 2006 debate, well-reasoned arguments were offered by a variety of tainted and untainted legislators for keeping taxes low, as well as raising them. But by October 2007 it was no secret to the public or legislators that Senator Ben Stevens had used the power of his position as Senate president to resist any rate over Murkowski's (and Bill Allen's) 20% rate. Senate Majority Leader Gene Therriault confided, "It finally got so unpleasant we just stopped having caucuses. He worked majority and minority votes out of the caucus."

And although the House eventually passed a twenty three and a half tax over the shenanigans of Bill Allen and his Corrupt Bastards Club members, House Speaker John Harris also conceded he knew the House would have to fold because Stevens was calling the shots. Harris said, "He shouldn't have had that power; no one person should. But they let him." So, by October 2007 the issue really wasn't whether the twenty two and a half rate was a fair and equitable compromise of widely divergent principled opinions, it was all about the perception of corruption and Governor Sarah Palin's skyrocketing popularity.

Palin's new plan was called Alaska's Clear and Equitable Share (ACES). It was meant to dovetail with her Alaska Gasline Inducement Act (AGIA), which the legislature had passed earlier that year to attract a pipeline developer. ACES called for a twenty five percent net tax to "stimulate new development and reinvestment in existing infrastructure." From the middle of October to the middle of November 2007, the legislature watched the battle of the oil industry consultants as they waged *PowerPoint* warfare in committee rooms throughout the capital. For legislators and staff, freedom of movement from forum to forum was historically unrestrained because of the conspicuous absence of oil industry and special interest lobbyists who customarily clog the main arteries of the capitol building.

When the House finally made the first move to adopt the governor's plan with only slight variation, the Anchorage conservative *Voice of the Times* editorial page howled:

> In the aftermath of the oil tax stampede in the Alaska House Sunday, we can only hope the state's economy is not well on its way to perdition. Lawmakers apparently desperate to prove they are not corrupt simps, as charged by Gov. Sarah Palin, voted 27 to 13 against the state's best interests. The sorry measure was sent to the Senate, where historically Alaska's adult lawmakers work. We can only hope they see this strong-armed robbery for what it is ---the work of folks who are afraid not to do the governor's bidding, even when it is wrong.

The Senate didn't. On the last day of the special session the Senate delivered back to the House an even more onerous version, accepting the House numbers and making the tax retroactive to June 30, 2007. The *Voice of the Times* immediately shot back,

> The decision by the Legislature to raise taxes on the oil industry was a bizarre act. That honorable body decided that last year's vote to increase taxes was tainted by corruption and the hike should be even higher. The bribery scandals wounded the state and the reputation of the Legislature, so its members decided to offset the damage by shooting themselves in the other foot. The folly of heaping a larger burden on oil production was telegraphed by the crowing of Senator Hollis French, one of the Legislature's most rabid liberal, green, anti-oil members. If that wasn't proof positive that the legislators were about to make a foolish move, then nothing could be. All its members who voted in favor of the tax boost should hang their heads.

The new legislation raised the base tax from twenty two and a half to twenty five percent of net profits, increased the *progressivity* (high oil price rate hike) rate from two to four percent, capped operating expense deductions for three years, authorized the state to write regulations to dictate what deductions are allowable and gave the state unprecedented discovery power to obtain information about oil industry operations.

Whether the tax increase chills oil industry investment in Alaska or was simply a high-stakes game of poker remains to be seen. But the subsequent announcement that *big three* oil giants ConocoPhillips and British Petroleum have teamed to build a natural gas pipeline seems to indicate who may have held the winning hand, a politically savvy young woman who is no longer just another pretty face.

"Serbia?" I said, "What's the FBI doing in Serbia? I thought that was CIA territory."

Kepner replied that Public Integrity Prosecutor Nick Marsh had invited her to co-instruct a week of ethics training for Serbian public officials. "Anyway, Frank, I'll be gone for a week, back for a few days and then I'm flying back East to spend Christmas with my mom. If anything case related comes up give Chad a call. You still have his numbers don't you? [I said I did] By the way, how are *you* doing?" I offered Kepner the usual platitudes, wished her happy holidays and ribbed her a little about the gargantuan moose mount I heard her husband stuck on their modest size living room wall for the holidays.

"Ol' Bullwinkle must be quite the designer statement," I said. She offered that if that was all it took to keep him happy, it was an oversized small price to pay and quickly changed the subject.

"Hey, I don't remember if I told you we agreed to extend the statute of limitations on Ted Stevens and we're talking to Cowdery and Clark [I whistled as she continued], so things are looking pretty good. I think 2008 will prove very interesting. Anyhow, Merry Christmas and tell your daughter I'll catch her when I get back if she's interested in knowing about the FBI academy. I can put her in touch with someone." I assured her my wife would be just thrilled and hung up.

Ethics Training. I remember asking Senator Dyson once if he supported the latest round of ethics code revisions for public officials. He said the question posed the same conundrum as asking me whether I've stopped beating my wife. I can't quite put my finger on it, but there's something odd about the need to codify values most of us presume are understood. I mean, my children may not have always behaved consistent with their values, but they didn't need a manual to know that lying, cheating, and stealing are wrong.

Up until a hundred years ago public officials in Western culture were heavily influenced by principles of natural law. They uniformly accepted that there are fundamental principles of right and wrong grounded in moral absolutes that, in a manner of speaking, compose a law above the law. Most people attributed the principles to divine revelation by the God of Jewish and Christian faith. A rather small minority acknowledged the absolute character of the principles, but took issue with the notion of a divine source. So in practice, legislators and jurists viewed themselves *law finders,* rather than *law makers.* They believed that if one could identify and apply moral truth to public affairs things would go better for the nation.

At the close of the Industrial Revolution, enlightened legislators and jurists all but abandoned natural law theory in favor of legal positivism. For the positivist, laws are valid if proffered in a procedurally correct manner by a recognized authority, regardless of moral implication. Positivists see no connection between law and ethics. As such, human affairs are governed by the majority vote of those in power at the moment and law is simply the vehicle used to accommodate a desired sociopolitical end. In effect, the highest laws of accountability are the laws passed by duly authorized legislative bodies, as upheld or modified by judicial interpretation and judgment. The only real question becomes who has the political stroke to decide the end to which the law adapts. The practical distinction today is that natural law oriented legislators and judges feel restrained by rules of law that are subject to a morality outside themselves and legal positivists believe the law they make is controlling authority regardless of personal notions of right and wrong.

Take religion, for example. Natural law leaning public officials view religion as a conservator of values which form a foundation for legislation. Positivists more often view religion and religious expression as a threat to freedom of choice, there's simply no room for a law above the law when truth is defined by majority vote. Since most positivists also believe the earth and our habitation thereon was by cosmic accident, it follows that the evolution of human thought and ideas must also be the accidental by-product of atomic energy, including the moral relativist cousin of positivism. I point this out only to suggest the improbability, in my mind, that a series of accidents could combine to form a reliable foundation for much of anything, let alone human governance. So it's no accident that I put my money on the existence of a law above the law that brought order out of chaos, as well as protects us from one another.

As a practical matter, most public officials probably don't pay much attention to the philosophical basis from which their decisions and the decisions of others emanate. And although that basis is always a matter of personal choice, when I find myself straddling the ethical fulcrum between teeter and totter I think about a story John W. Montgomery used to tell: *There was once a rabbit of philosophical temperament that invited a politically oriented fox to dinner. During the entrée, the rabbit presented an interesting argument on the relativity of all law and morals, stressing that each beast, in the final analysis, has a right to his own legal system. Now the fox didn't find the argument entirely convincing on the in- tellectual level, but he was much impressed with its practicality. For dessert he ate the rabbit Lapin a la Crème.*

The moral, of course, is that philosophical viewpoints are of immense (and often predictable) practical consequence. That certainly appears to be the case in the rapidly expanding membership of the Corrupt Bas- tards Club, so I find it doubtful that mandatory *ethics* training would have made much of a difference. After all, prisons are full of people who know right from wrong but for a variety of reasons chose the lat- ter, or believed they had a right to redefine the law to meet a personal end, but didn't have the political stroke to get away with it.

Yet Kepner raised another more disturbing question before she left for Serbia, a question I had been struggling with. She asked how I was doing? A simple question, on its face, but in my mind it was *FBI-speak* for, *Frank, if you had it to do over, would you still agree to help us?* You see, none of us expected to celebrate our four-year anniversary still trolling for the big fish. Kepner knew the price for my family and me had been high and implied as much one day in a rare, reflective mo- ment when she rhetorically asked, "So how does it feel to be screwed by the government." With a break in the action, maybe it was time to think about it.

After my cover was exposed in the Anderson case there was a lot of speculation about my role in the dramatically evolving expose of po- litical corruption in Alaska. Other than the press release acknowledg- ing that I was, indeed, CS-1 and had been working for the government since spring 2004, I studiously avoided conversations with the press and anyone else about the corruption investigations. I was concerned about letting something slip that would compromise a case or influence an upcoming trial. But silence has a price. It allows the opposition, spectators, and speculators to control the dialogue and influence perception.

To their credit, U.S. Attorney Joe Bottini gave fair warning that I was the key witness in the first few corruption cases, so if any of them ended up in trial, anonymity was not an option. He also warned that the defense would try to skew a five-year-old improper campaign contribution (a fleeting moment of stupid that could have resulted in a state fine equivalent to a parking ticket) and thirteen-year-old personal loan from Weimar to look like the basis for a secret plea deal exchanged for testimony against their clients. He wrapped up saying, "on the other hand, the cases are so strong they aren't likely to go to trial." Well, go to trial they did. But Bottini was mostly correct.

The evidence in the first three cases was so overwhelming the only defense was, indeed, to impugn the integrity of the government witnesses, whether co-defendants (which wasn't hard), federal officials, or the Confidential Source. I was the primary government source and the first case hinged on the credibility of my testimony. So, as anticipated, Anderson's frustrated and desperate defense attorney sneered in closing, "You set up Tom Anderson to keep yourself out of his seat, didn't you?"

I replied, "No."

So he pressed on, "You were under investigation, weren't you?"

I replied, "Yes, the project I…"

He interrupted, "Just answer the question! Yes, or no? Were you or weren't you under investigation by the FBI?"

I replied, "Yes, I was."

Smiling at the jury he said he had no other questions and thanked me, implying I entrapped Anderson to stay out of trouble.

The Federal Prosecutor then stood and asked, "Mr. Prewitt, has the government ever made any promises to you?"

I replied, "No."

He followed, "Did you assist the government voluntarily, without coercion?"

I said yes and explained I knew I was at no risk and they needed my help. The local press covered the defense questions and my replies, selectively ignoring the government's clarifying rebuttal and leaving the impression I was only helping the government to save my skin.

Not to be outdone, two months later Kohring's defense attorney flailed his arms and theatrically asked the jury how they could possibly believe the testimony of a "sleazy lobbyist" who was in trouble and "cut a deal to save his own neck." After closing arguments U.S. Attorney Bottini had had enough, summoned mainstream reporters and said, "*Nothing* can be further from the truth. Prewitt has done a tremendous job for the government. We owe him a lot, frankly." But Bottini wasn't at liberty to elaborate.

I understand why defense attorneys and reporters characterize players and events the way they do; we all have to eat and pay bills. But without ethical restraint, lawyering and reporting degenerate into self-serving manipulation of whatever means are needed to reach the desired result. Intentional or not, truth becomes a mere tool in the box of tactics assembled to achieve a strategic end. Truth be told, lawyering and reporting based on compromised truth yanks threads from the frayed fabric that still protects freedom of speech and our pursuit of life, liberty, and happiness.

Unlike the pragmatic and ethically challenged fox, the integrity of our legal system is based on the telling of truth, *the whole truth, and nothing but the truth.* The establishment of truth ensures and protects both the obligations and benefits we all enjoy in a free society. Truth is so important there are grave sanctions in our legal system for failure to tell the truth. And the truth I was struggling with (and Kepner well understood) was that no one would have known about my meetings with the government if I had said, "Thanks, but no thanks!" to helping the FBI in their quest to expose and prosecute political corruption. But declining their request was simply not an option I could live with, let's just call it a matter of personal ethics.

What the government didn't prepare me for was the price tag on silence. I wasn't emotionally prepared to become free pickin's for an information-starved press, the venomous speculation of bloggers, strutting defense attorneys' sneering innuendo, criminal defendants and families' self-serving lies, and the holy host of predatory, self-righteous Monday-morning commentators.

You see, unlike the constitutional *due process* afforded the criminal defendants, public perception of my role and motivation was shaped with no protective process and based entirely on media fixation on defense attorneys' sneering innuendo of criminal wrongdoing and a "hide-saving secret plea deal." But, as the saying goes, "no good deed goes unpunished," because once the die of innuendo is cast on the not-so-fair and not-so-balanced worldwide web, the intended target bears the *Mark of the Scarlet Google* for all to see and wonder. After all, who in their right mind would make that kind of sacrifice if they hadn't been coerced, or had nothing to lose by looking the other way?

And the cost? For a couple of years (while the cases were still covert) I had to terminate or decline a half dozen consulting and executive-level employment opportunities to avoid compromising the investigations, all while donating over a thousand hours of counsel, analysis, and active participation in undercover operations. But the real price of participation hit after my role went public and a friend politely suggested I was now too "radioactive" as a result of publicity to assume, presume, or resume past affiliations and expectations. That's lawyer-speak for, "It's okay Frankie, just kiss off your career and find something else to do." And he was correct.

In the heat of events I guess I hadn't noticed (or didn't want to notice) that phone calls from past friends and affiliates were becoming exceedingly rare; my previously active social calendar was quite open; and my wife and I seemed to be having more conversations about personal safety and our uncertain future. So when Kepner asked, "How are you doin' Frank?" I guess I should have said, "*Frankly Scarlet, not worth a damn*! My mother died during the Anderson trial; my bank account's tapped; I have a bad case of professional leprosy; one kid left in college; and I'm coming up on my fifth anniversary with the FBI......*how 'bout you, sweetheart?*"

Fortunately, I'm not James Cagney and that's not how I feel. But thanks for taking a break in the story to let me vent. I don't want to minimize the sacrifice or the stress, but my wife and I are actually honored that we were able to help clean up a political custom and culture mess that our kids and their friends don't deserve to inherit.

Consider, for example, just one socioeconomic impact: As you recall, Governor Palin called a special legislative session in October 2007 to reconsider the PPT tax passed the year before. In 2006, the Corrupt Bastards Club fought tooth and nail for a twenty percent tax. Other legislators were fighting for a twenty five percent rate, or higher. The tainted 2006 compromise tax ended up at twenty two and a half percent (this sounds boring, but stay with me). Expert testimony projected a one hundred fifty million dollar annual increase in State revenue for every one percentage point above the Oil Industry's desired twenty percent tax rate.

In the 2007 Special Legislative Session Democrats and Republicans (with one exception) *unanimously* voted to raise the tax another two and a half percent to twenty five percent.. The untainted two and a half percent bump will increase Alaska State revenue by three hundred seventy five million dollars per year, *nearly two billion dollars over the next five years!* Was the tax hike good public policy? Time will tell. The important thing is that it was fair and open public policy. If I had turned down Kepner, in all probability the State would not be receiving the increased revenue. More important, the Corrupt Bastards Club would still be in full operation undermining the public process, and our Constitutional right to honest representation and fair debate.

For reasons I don't understand, exposing Alaska's custom and culture of political corruption seemed to require Kepner's and my combined catalytic chemistry to activate the tidal wave of contributions that would eventually expose the full extent of the disease. So, in retrospect, "Yes Kepner, I guess I would choose to do it all again, though I'm not so sure our choices have that much to do with destiny." But next time I'd insist that the FBI change a few things, like the location of body wires, who springs for lunch, Chad's attitude (*just kidding*), and how to keep a confidential source, well, *CONFIDENTIAL,* they do it all the time in the movies!

So I'm wrapping up this chapter because it's December 14, 2007 and our youngest returns from her first college semester away from home tonight. Our other kids and some close friends who have no Alaska family will be joining us for the holidays and we're gonna do stuff twenty and thirty-somethings do, you know, zip lines, snow balls, terrible music, food, beer, gifts, and some count-your-blessings time.

Kepner flew out to Serbia yesterday. I don't expect to hear from her until after the holidays, but I imagine Chad will drop by for a checkup and free cup of coffee. I think about Anderson, Kohring, Kott and the others quite a bit and pray for them and their loved ones in that awkward way Jesus told us all to pray for each other, our enemies, our leaders and especially, I suppose, our *used-to-be* leaders, because for some it was a long, hard landing. And they were just the low-hanging fruit. So see you next -

Okay. I can't do it. I just can't end the year on a somber note. So, you wanna know the top ten ways to recognize an Alaska politician? Sure you do.

You Know You're With A Politician From Alaska When

10. the fundraiser beverage is brew and shots and entertainment is a bug zapper;

9. biographical research reveals a family tree with no branches;

8. the guy at the next table keeps adjusting his shirt button;

7. *CBC* embossed on a ball cap doesn't stand for Conservative Baptist Church;

6. earmarks are grants from the Federally Entitled Crony Enactments (*FECES*);

5. *Bridges To Nowhere* are bridges to a relative's land development;

4. pork of any cut is the favored meat of the day;

3. the rest of the world is *outside* (see, Glossary);

2. which leaf makes the best toilet paper is appropriate dinner conversation; and

1. dinner ends with a round of Oosik jokes (see, Glossary).

Fortunately the corruption shoe only fit a small handful of Alaska politicians, so a special thanks to my friends in public service who still have a sense of humor.

Chapter Eight
Trolling For Winter Kings

I mentioned earlier that U.S. Senator Ted Stevens' official residence is in Girdwood, Alaska, a small community that also hosts the annual U.S. Alpine National Ski Championships. Every few years the Alyeska Ski Resort taunts monster-thigh athletes from around the country into a game of chicken with 2,550 vertical feet of eye-popping, knee-jarring, heart-pounding splendor. From her sea level base to 4,000-foot summit, Mount Alyeska is an extreme skier paradise. The resort is a twisting forty mile drive from Anchorage, south, along Turnagain Arm and I was headed there to have lunch with Special Agent Chad Joy.

Turnagain Arm separates mainland Alaska from the Kenai Peninsula and was named by Captain Cook's sailing master, William Bligh, of HMS Bounty fame. A cranky Captain Cook was on his third and final attempt to find the Northwest Passage when he spotted the huge inlet. He ordered an expedition that grew so frustrated by tide, current, wind, and mud flats, it returned to the mother ship with a, "No passage, sir." Frustrated, Captain Cook ordered Master Bligh to finish the job. He did, reported there was just a river at the other end and named the inlet, "Turn*again* Arm." I imagine Bligh's expletives dropped off when the name transitioned from oral to written history. But, as history would have it, destiny was waiting for the future *Capt'n* Bligh to have his own bad day at sea.

The drive along Turnagain Arm is one of the most spectacular sights in the world. Mountains on both sides of the long inlet shoot 5,000 feet from sea level to glacier-capped summit in a revolving seasonal kaleidoscope of glacial winter blue, emerald summer green and flaming fingers of fall. The highway itself is brutally carved out of the granite mountain range base and meanders along the waterline offering unparalleled sensuous displays of sight and sound.

During summer the *Arm* flows through cobalt and magenta fields of fireweed and lupin playing host to world record tides and a rare tidal bore. The bore tide can reach 6 feet high and travel the 50 mile length of the inlet in one massive, cresting wave at 15 miles per hour. From the highway thrilled tourists watch thrill-seeking surfers and kayakers ride the bore wave for miles chased by frenzied hooligan tail-dancing out of the path of grinning, white-faced beluga whale, a thrilling sight unless, of course, you miss it because you're too mesmerized by Dall sheep performing cliff-hanging photo-ops on the other side of the road.

I headed south down the *Arm* to meet Chad on a sparkling New Year's winter day. Along the highway, glacial springs and mountain run-off formed towering crystal ice sculptures that clung tenaciously to the face of the winding granite wall corridor. Every few miles a blue translucent ice cathedral played host to devout Patagonian robed pilgrims suspended by rainbow ropes, struggling under the weight of sole thorns and jangling paraphernalia, chanting, picking, and grinning their way to resplendent heights. One hundred feet below, sharp-eyed disciples scurried about untangling lines, shouting warnings and preparing the post-ascension communion of granola and Alaskan Amber micro brew. As I passed the climbers I had to admit I don't really understand the *extreme sports* mentality, yet I humbly realized that today I was also on a pilgrimage, a journey to meet with Special Agent Kepner's partner: FBI grand cynic and master investigator, Chad Joy.

Chad is a close-cropped, conservatively attired, thirty-something with penetrating blue eyes and the wit of a leprechaun on steroids. A humorist and practical joker, when he's not busy persecuting his peers with startling revelations of twisted, one-off, side splitting impropriety, he tends to his true calling: busting the bad guys. By 2006, the investigation had grown to the point where Kepner had to delegate or drown. In particular, the younger Stevens' fisheries cases were taking on a disturbing briar patch appearance requiring special pruning skills and Special Agent Joy was just the man for the job.

Chad was at Girdwood tending some loose ends in the senior Stevens' investigation and wanted to pick my brain on some technical information about operating boats in Alaska's treacherous offshore waters. Evidently something in the junior Stevens' mariner techno-speak had tweaked an antenna in Chad's ever suspicious mind, so we agreed to meet for lunch at Chair 5, a quiet little pub where no one would notice or overhear us. When I entered the pub Chad was already blending into a corner table with a tall, chilled (root) beer, black boots, black ball cap, black Kevlar vest and the discreet black butt of a 9mm Glock. I walked around a pool table, sat down, and said, "We're in a family ski resort Chad, not a scene out of the *Bourne Ultimatum*, nice outfit."

Chad smiled, ignored my observation and said, "Great, Frank. How are you?"

Chad had some navigation questions about compensating for wind, tide, and current, the difference between displacement hulls and planing hulls, and general reliability of weather forecasts in the Gulf of Alaska. Even though I was a confidential source, Kepner and Chad always took extreme care not to say more about the investigations than necessary to achieve their information goal. But as we munched, sipped, and talked away the early afternoon, it wasn't difficult to connect the dots between what I already knew about former Alaska senator Ben Stevens and a very deep pile of kimshe. And I wasn't alone.

By 2008 the local press, bloggers and anyone else paying attention knew the younger Stevens' case was serious and could take the government a long time to process. This was confirmed by a status report filed January 31, 2008 by Public Integrity Unit attorneys requesting that the court postpone sentencing Bill Allen and Rick Smith indefinitely because "the current investigation is exceedingly complex due to a variety of issues and is ongoing." They recommended another "status report" in April, but it was the timing of the other cases that was drawing most of the attention and the immediate concern was Senator John Cowdery.

Ever since VECO Rick Smith testified that he had bribed him, rumors of Cowdery's various acts and omissions circled the air like flies over an outhouse with calls for resignation hounding his every move, that is, until he was hospitalized with an undisclosed condition one week before the 2008 legislative session. Earlier in the week Cowdery had announced that he *would not* resign because of the corruption probe and *would not* be attending the 2008 session for health reasons, but *would* cover his senatorial duties by phone. Seizing Cowdery's moment of profound arrogance, the day before the legislature gaveled into session party leaders and district officials passed a resolution urging Cowdery to step down because his physical absence would *disenfranchise the voters of this district on most issues of importance.*

The next day, one hour before the governor's State of the State address, Cowdery resigned as chair of the Senate Rules Committee saying, *Due to my recurrent health issues I have decided it's best for me and the Alaska Senate to resign as chairman of the Senate Rules Committee. When my health allows it I will return to Juneau as quickly as possible so I can work on the issues that are important to the people of my Senate District.*

I heard Cowdery's announcement while reading about the denial of former House Speaker Pete Kott's request to postpone reporting to Federal prison so he could be around for the birth of a grandchild. After the fall 2007 conviction, Kott was granted two requests to travel outside Alaska before sentencing. The first was a trip to Mesquite, Nevada with his girlfriend, to reportedly visit her family. The second was to use up an old airline ticket to Las Vegas (kind of makes you wonder where he would be right now if he'd hit a jackpot). Patience exhausted at yet a third request, federal prosecutors howled that it was high time for Kott to face the consequences of his actions. Judge Sedwick agreed and Kott finally reported to the Federal Penitentiary at Sheridan, Oregon on January 17, 2008, four months of freedom after his conviction. I put down the paper, shook my head and thought, "These guys really don't get it."

Cowdery's impending indictment and powerful position as Senate Rules chair was a real concern to the governor, legislature and most Alaskans, but 2008 was also a presidential election year and the far greater concern was that U.S. Senator Ted Stevens and U.S. Congressman Don Young were both up for reelection. As Young told the *Anchorage Daily News* in late May 2008, "I am running and I am running hard. We live in a world where liberals from San Francisco are running Congress and their greatest wish is to turn Alaska into a national park. Well, that's not happening on my watch…Senator Stevens and I have run together all these years and we'll be running together this year. The Senator's the God Father of Alaska and I'm his Lieutenant." I guess that about says it all.

By the time Young and Stevens announced their 2008 reelection campaigns, the political corruption investigations had left most Alaskans questioning whether the two could effectively continue to serve the state and the nation. Though Democrats took it a bit further, salivating behind thinly veiled enthusiasm over a real shot at the congressional seats. But there was also a small problem. Alaskans understand that wounded predators are vulnerable, and vulnerable predators are dangerous, *and* unpredictable. For Republicans and Democrats the strategic question was: How long could they afford to wait before sending new *Davids* into the ring with the wounded and angry old *Goliaths*?

The way things were shaping up, I figured indictments or plea deals on John Cowdery and Jim Clark (former governor Murkowski's chief of staff) were right around the corner, the shoe would probably drop on Senators father and son Stevens by mid-summer or fall and the case building against *Congressman For All Alaska* Don Young would slide past the August 2008 primary elections, and that was a big problem. With public uncertainty over pending indictments, massive competing egos, and the sheer magnitude of the congressional veterans' campaign war chests, political strategists and prognosticators were seriously concerned about the possibility of a statewide epidemic of *Republican Electile Dysfunction*: the inability to become aroused by any candidate (an ironically arousing thought to Alaska's congressionally impotent democrats).

Then there were the cases sitting on federal ice for lack of immediate concern or stature. Alaska Senator Donny Olson, for example, was named in the Kott trial as the senator that John Cowdery *could deliver* for a mere twenty five thousand dollar contribution; investigations into former Alaska senator Jerry Ward and multimillionaire businessman Bill Weimar had been completed at least a year before; political cash handouts from Alaska fur-trading entrepreneur Perry Green were burning a hole in prosecutors' pockets; former representative Bruce Weyhrauch's trial was stalled on a procedural appeal; former representative Beverly Masek's alleged *quid pro quo* relationship with Bill Allen and Perry Green was approaching the statute of limitations limit for prosecution; the lingering charges against the remaining VECO executives were simmering on a back burner; and a small handful of residual affiliations could prove up after the cooperators' cooperation. Talk about herding chickens.

Curious over the extraordinary period of time it was taking to bring the growing number of cases to justice, I asked one of the U.S. Attorneys why the government didn't sweep up the whole gang with mass arrests, rather than drag the cases on for years. Interestingly, she said it was a *right to speedy trial* issue and explained that even though several investigations were complete, most corruption cases have a five-year statute of limitations. She said that this meant the Feds could continue to expand investigations without the distraction of trial preparation, which consumes huge resources and months of DOJ staff time.

Once an arrest is made, or an indictment issued, the clock on a federal defendant's right to a speedy trial starts running. The running clock then triggers a right to discover confidential information which can, and often does, compromise ongoing investigations. Experienced defense attorneys also press for an immediate trial date, hoping to catch the government unprepared and force a favorable offer. So, as it turns out, it's common federal practice to sit on cases until it's convenient or expedient to make an arrest. I conceded to the logic, and with five fingers realized that the discovery of crimes committed in 2003 and 2004 (when this whole thing started) didn't technically have to be charged until 2008 and 2009. And there, I guess, was the answer to my question, though lawyers do have a way of explaining things so we're never quite sure.

———

The caller ID on my phone blinked *Anchorage FBI*. I picked up the phone, "Frank here."

A female voice on the other end said, "Hey, I'm back."

I recognized Kepner's voice and asked how the trip to Serbia went.

She said it was real interesting. The ethics classes went well and a tour of Belgrade was terrific, except for anti-American sentiment over bombings that had occurred ten years before. After a little more small talk she said, "Frank, can we meet tomorrow for coffee?" She sounded odd and we agreed to meet the next day at Kaladi Brothers on Huffman Road in Anchorage at 8:30 a.m.

I arrived at the café a few minutes early, ordered an *Americano with room* and found a quiet table where we could talk without being overheard. Kepner arrived a few minutes later, poured a regular cup of coffee and asked how things were going. I told her about our family holiday festivities, the weather and a few other mundane things, angling for her to get to the real reason we were meeting. After a couple rounds of small talk she said she wanted to tell me about a meeting with her supervisor. "Remember the lunch we had before I left?" I nodded and she went on, "Well, someone else at the table saw the picture of the dog portrait your wife gave me for Christmas and expressed concern."

I interrupted, "Concern about what?"

She said, "Concern about accepting a gift from a Confidential Source. It gives the appearance we may be too close."

I laughed and said, "Well that's easy, why don't you pay for it, we can use the dough!"

She replied, "No, serious, it's a problem."

"What's a problem?" I said.

"The appearance, idiot!" she replied.

I thought for a moment, looked real concerned, and said, "You mean we're breaking up?"

Finally she laughed and explained that there was some kind of incident with an agent back in Baltimore who got too close to a source and ended up embarrassing the Bureau.

I studied her for a moment and said, "Let me get this straight. I worked covert operations with you and your team nearly full-time for two years, worked overt, including trials, for another two, and someone's concerned we might be too close!?" I squinted, leaned forward and cynically whispered, "Has anyone told my wife?"

Kepner replied, "Oh come on, there was just concern over the portrait and a *word to the wise*."

I settled down a little and said, "Ahh, *wise words*. I like wise words. Come on Kepner, once you figured out I wasn't a crook you know very well we both had to trust each other to do what we've accomplished. If I hadn't thought you really cared about me, my family, and getting to the real source of the corruption, I would have been out of here a long time ago. The first week we met I said I thought you were on to something, but you were looking under the wrong rocks. Remember? [Kepner nodded] When you say my help was *"indispensable"* I take you at your word, but without a trusting r-e-l-a-t-i-o-n-s-h-i-p we wouldn't be sitting here today, and the *Corrupt Bastards Club* might still be recruiting members."

Kepner looked me straight in the eyes and said, "You're over-react-ing. You know these cases are fragile and there can't be even a whiff of impropriety!"

I avoided her stare, took a sip of coffee and mumbled, "Well, that's easy because there hasn't been and won't be."

In truth, we had become very close. People have real lives, real feelings, real highs, and real lows. Some people bring out our best, others our worst. Some relationships fit like a glove, others chafe like a scouring pad. Most of us are healthiest and happiest in circles of mutually supportive community. And for all those very natural reasons Kepner and I worked well together. So I grudgingly agreed that a little reminder wasn't a bad thing, settled down and said, "Vicki painted pet portraits for a bunch of family, friends, and acquaintances at Christmas and *I'm* the one who asked *you* for a photograph of your dog because Vicki supposedly needed a good likeness of a yellow lab for her art group."

Kepner nodded and I continued, "The going commercial rate is a few hundred bucks. Why don't you just go over to her studio and cut a check, she'll give you a receipt and everything will be squeaky clean. But when these cases are all closed I want an invitation to one of your in-service training classes to talk about agent-source relations from the *source* side of things." Kepner looked puzzled, so I explained, "I understand Bureau concern over conflicts of interest. But extreme cases make poor general policy. It was your training and *humanity* that accomplished the government's mission. Robotons don't have instincts or feelings, that's why they make crappy supervisors and can't solve cases, they also make lousy friends."

Kepner smiled, paid for her own coffee and said, "Catch ya later, I'm late for a meeting downtown with Robocop." I smiled, waved goodbye and thought, "What a paranoid outfit! They hire terrific people, put them through incredible training, and then force them to look over their shoulders in a defensive atmosphere of suspicion and distrust. Then again, they *are* spies, maybe that's why they're so good at what they do." So I shredded the draft complaint in my mind and was letting the pieces blow away when I saw Kepner turn and head back to my table.

"Say Frank," she said, "I almost forgot to tell you I'm tying up loose ends on the Ted Stevens investigation. As soon as it goes public Ward's antennae are gonna start twitching." Kepner looked around to make sure no one was headed in our direction, sat down, and continued.

"I'd like to get Weimar's help to strengthen the case against Ward. He's got a hot temper. How would you go about getting his cooperation?"

I thought for a moment and said, "Act quick." Kepner looked puzzled and I continued, "Weimar's dumped a bunch of money into his estate at Big Arm, Montana. He's got 50 acres and a mansion that overlooks Flathead Lake. He's turning it into kind of a spa resort and putting it up for sale next month for twenty million dollars. Then he's moving onto his new yacht in Seattle and heading North to cruise Alaska for the summer before heading to Mexico."

Kepner asked, "How do you know what he's up to?"

I smiled and said, "I just know things." She gave me that familiar look, so I continued.

"Weimar called a couple of weeks ago and told me about his travel plans. He needed help setting up a trip itinerary for Prince William Sound. You know, stuff to see, where to anchor, distance between way-points, how to avoid rocks, that kind of thing. If I were you I'd go have a little chat before he sells the Montana property, dumps the money in an offshore account and morphs into a wandering yacht gypsy. Knowing Weimar, he's real leveraged right now. You show up at his door with convincing evidence his goose is cooked and I think he'll make a calculated business decision."

Kepner looked interested and said, "What do you mean?"

I continued, "Weimar is 68 years old and he's always whining about life being a cosmic joke. He's paranoid about getting old, feeble, and dependent and worships money as life's only source of happiness and security. The around-the-world yacht junket is his last *hurrah*. He plans to travel for as long as his health holds out and, hopefully, cross the great cosmic divide between known and unknown before he's, as he puts it, 'in diapers.' My guess is he'll kill himself playing chicken with a hundred-ton ocean freighter long before he has to worry about diapers.

You're actually doing him a favor. The way he eats and navigates prison will probably extend his life. But if you insist on his cooperation I would talk to him about Tom and Bill."

Kepner raised an eyebrow and asked, "Anderson and Bobrick?"

I said, "Yeah. Think about it. Tom Anderson told you to shove it and he got five years in prison, with five years' probation for selling his office for chump change. Bobrick was the mastermind and coconspirator in the deal. He cooperated with you and got a measly five months at a minimum-security golf resort and five months of home confinement. Anderson didn't know when or where you would strike. Bobrick got to recommend where he would go and you worked with him on timing."

Kepner looked thoughtful and asked, "So you think Weimar will want time to organize his affairs?"

I replied, "That's my bet. I think he's smart enough to know that if you pop him in the next month or two he'll lose control and might lose his fortune. If you promise to recommend a reduced sentence and offer some timing flexibility and predictability in exchange for cooperation, I think he'll handle it like a business decision instead of his usual explosively litigious self. You'll just have to convince him your case is a slam-dunk. I figure you've got a four to six week window."

Kepner said, "Well, why don't you give him a call and see when he's leaving for Seattle. I think I'd rather talk to him at his home in Montana. Got any other ideas?"

I thought for a moment and replied, "Well, I'm still frosted that Weimar's mud splashed all over me, but I still like the guy. I'd be happy to send a personal note vouching for you, explaining my role and urging him to cooperate."

Kepner said she was heading to Washington DC for a week and would give it some thought. She stood, grabbed her things, thanked me for the help and headed downtown a bit late for her "already late" meeting. I watched her leave, tossed a half-eaten scone and the empty cups into a trash can, took a deep drag off the roasting beans and followed, wondering how Weimar was going to react.

(You know, writing a book as events unfold is a surreal experience. While I was sitting at my computer telling you about Kepner's plan to intercept Weimar, guess who called? Yep, Weimar. We had a nice chat about his upcoming trip to Alaska. He wanted some more information about Prince William Sound and the Kenai Fjords and said the trip is still on schedule. He plans to move onto the new yacht in early April and head north at the end of the month through British Columbia to Ketchikan on the first leg of the journey. Life's interesting, you just never know what might be lurking around the next corner.)

"Get up! We're gonna be late. I'm so excited. Emmy, go kiss dad, go on, go kiss dad." I groaned as 60 pounds of fur, slobber, and morning breath excitedly pounced at my wife's command. Vicki's a dog lover and I've grown accustomed to the unusual practice among her breed of attributing human qualities to four legged creatures. Not to say they aren't better company than, say, most 12-year-olds, I just don't think it's right to mislead them about their lineage. But this morning is the start of the world-famous Iditarod Trail Sled Dog race and I was about to be overruled by a howling mob of fur-bearing creatures of both species, in spite of the grimacing fact it was so cold out Starbucks was serving coffee on a stick.

The Iditarod kicks off on the last day of Fur Rendezvous, which began when fur trappers gathered in Anchorage to sell their winter harvests, take a bath, and reacquaint themselves with civilization. It's the Alaska equivalent of carnival: seven days and nights packed with fireworks, a miners' and trappers' ball, snow sculpting, figure skating, dog weight pulls, and the world renowned Running of the Reindeer, where one thousand men and women flee down the streets of Anchorage chased by a licking, nudging, wet-nose-sliming herd of reindeer bumping, grinding, and pooping their way to feed buckets of grain and photo ops.

The Iditarod is known as the Last Great Race on Earth and is comparable to no other similar event in the world. On March 1, 2008, ninety six teams of twelve to sixteen dogs and a musher set out on a 1,150 mile journey from Anchorage to Nome. The race takes ten to seventeen days, depending on conditions. And oh, the conditions! In a relentless, twenty-four-hour nonstop journey, with one 24 and two 8 hour mandatory rest periods, men, women, and dogs "Mush!", "Hike!", "Gee!", and "Haw!" their way over jagged mountain ranges, across frozen rivers, and up the windswept coast in below-zero temperature, blizzards, and pitch black darkness. They pass through Cripple or Shageluk, then on to Unalakleet, Shaktoolik, Koyuk, White Mountain, and on to Nome where every finishing competitor receives a hero's welcome for simply completing the grueling event. Many don't make it.

In any other year the Iditarod would have dominated headlines for the first few days of the race. Not 2008. I had just regained feeling in my toes and other extremities when another mukluk dropped. I wasn't surprised. I'd been hopeful that Kepner had succeeded in a cooperation agreement, but it was a sobering moment nonetheless when I picked up the morning paper and read the headline:

Anchorage Daily News
March 4, 2008
By Richard Mauer and Sean Cockerham

Former Murkowski Aide Pleads Guilty

Jim Clark, once at the heart of power as former Gov. Frank Murkowski's Chief of Staff, became a contrite, convicted felon Tuesday as he pleaded guilty to a federal conspiracy charge stemming from an illegal effort to re-elect his boss in 2006.

The silver-haired Clark, an attorney and lobbyist by trade, entered his plea before U.S. District Court Judge John Sedwick, then turned himself over to U.S. Marshalls to be booked, fingerprinted and have his mug shot taken.

"I've got a lot of atonement to do," Clark, 64, said as he stopped to speak with reporters on his way out of the courthouse...His sentencing will be delayed at least six months while he demonstrates his cooperation with ongoing investigations.

Clark pleaded guilty to conspiring with former officials of VECO...to secretly channel $68,550 from VECO into Murkowski's re-election effort...Clark told reporters he never told Murkowski about the VECO assistance.

When Assistant U. S. Attorney James Goeke finished reading the underlying facts of the case, (Judge) Sedwick asked Clark if they were true. "With great anguish and remorse, I admit that they are," Clark said. "And how do you plead?" the Judge asked. "I plead guilty, your Honor."

Clark faces five years in prison and a $250,000 fine, but the government said his contrition and assistance could knock off more than a year off his time and eliminate most of the fine.

While the plea and contrition stunned Alaska (and was of reporting interest to the *New York Times* and other national publications), the most intriguing detail of the surprise consolidated hearing was in the closing paragraphs of the *Factual Basis For Plea* signed by Clark and filed with his plea agreement:

James Clark acknowledges that the statements and admissions contained in the foregoing Factual Basis for Plea do not constitute all of the facts relevant to the matters discussed herein, nor do the foregoing paragraphs contain a complete discussion of the acts taken by Clark and/or his co-conspirators. Instead, Clark understands that this Factual Basis for Plea is merely a summary of some, but not all, criminal conduct engaged in by Clark. Clark further understands that he may be required at future proceedings to provide further and more complete details of the matters discussed herein.

I thought *merely a summary, but not all the criminal conduct by Clark and/or his co-conspirators*, bet there are some sweaty palms in high places tonight, and put down the paper.

———————

One week before Easter the Kepner bunny delivered a basket of eggs to Bill Weimar at his home in Big Arm, Montana. He didn't seem particularly surprised to make her acquaintance and she said he was actually quite hospitable as she laid out the case against him and the desire for cooperation in the case against former senator Ward and others. They agreed to meet again after he retained counsel and bid each other a pleasant day.

Successful, but kind of anticlimactic, Kepner drove back to Missoula, hopped a flight to Seattle and arrived just in time to board an Alaska Airlines milk run to Anchorage. It had been a busy month of meetings in Washington DC trying to wrap up affairs on Ted Stevens and Don Young, but overall she was pleased. All the cases were progressing well, including the younger Stevens', and Kepner was actually looking forward to handing the cooperators' spinoff and back-burner cases to some of the new agents. There'd be a couple of years of oversight minutia, plea deals, some trial testimony, and inevitable unforeseen emergencies, but for the first time in years she could see the light at the end of the tunnel, and it was bright. The steady drone of the jet engines were clouding her mind, so Kepner leaned back, closed her eyes and fell asleep wondering if the Bureau had any openings someplace warm and tropical.

———•———

The final approach on the long flight from anywhere to Anchorage is an exhilarating experience. After hours of high-altitude cruising, docile, drone-drunk passengers wince as overhead speakers order flight attendants to prepare for landing. Seat belts on, seat backs forward, tray tables up, and another radio check confirm that the weary, seat-sore passengers are all secure. Then it happens. Within moments an invisible force hijacks the cockpit, seizes manual control and rudely snaps the lethargic aircraft from automated slumber into a steep, banking plunge over Mount Alyeska and into the airspace above Turnagain Arm.

In a stomach-clutching descent, glacier-tipped mountains suddenly materialize off each wingtip and whisk out of sight as the airborne bobsled plummets down the narrow, misty, fjord. With the finish line in sight, the jet bursts over the Arm, banks sharply over Fire Island and heads straight for a vertical rock wall rising one hundred feet out of the choppy, frigid waters of Cook Inlet. Bobbing, weaving, and precariously levitating between land and sea, rubber and asphalt finally kiss as white-knuckled passengers break out in spontaneous applause over spectacular scenery and the precious gift of life. Many board cruise ships for the return passage.

I was watching what may have been Kepner's incoming flight from a wind-swept mountain perch, thinking about how far the ripple effect of political corruption might extend, when I had a reflective moment. Seated above a snow-packed gully, enjoying the sweeping view across the Inlet, I picked up a small rock and chucked it out into space. The rock didn't make it through the earth's gravitational pull and began a slow, arching descent until it pierced the snowpack with a barely audible *ka-thunk*. Within seconds I heard a low groan and felt the earth beneath my seat shiver as the tranquil, sparkling snowpack transformed into a violent, plunging mass of rock and ice. I sat mesmerized by the awesome scene and wondered, "Why me?" Why didn't Kepner pick up a different rock, they were all over the place. When I agreed to allow the insignificant rock of my life to be chucked out over the snowpack we didn't have a clue it would trigger a political avalanche of epic proportions. A vibrating cell phone interrupted my thoughts. It was a message from Kepner telling me she was back, things went well with Weimar, and asking whether I could come downtown for a few minutes between ten and eleven the next morning.

I could see the airport from my mountain perch and wondered whether she was calling from the plane that just landed. I dialed, but there was no answer, so I left a message that I'd be there at ten and to let me know if there was anything to bring. I hiked back to my car and headed home wondering, "What now?"

At ten a.m. the next morning I parked across the street from Weimar's old office and smiled, recalling him whisper *but that would be wrong* into his lampshade. I entered the discreet, street-level public entry to FBI Regional Headquarters and was just refilling my pockets from the security bucket when Kepner opened a door and waved me in.

"So it worked!" I said.

"Yeah. He was quite jovial, even showed us around the mansion and asked how the other cases were coming." Our voices bounced off the concrete walls as we climbed the stairs to Kepner's office.

"You're kidding?" I said.

Kepner laughed and replied, "No, really. You were right on target. A light really went on when I talked about his ol' buddy Bobrick getting such a light sentence and personal planning time for cooperating."

I smiled and asked, "So how'd the follow-up meeting go?"

Kepner shook her head, gave me a mystified grin and said, "It went great! He said he's gonna take full responsibility and take his medicine. Of course, hearing his conversations with Ward and seeing the evidence of the cash exchanges helped a lot."

I chuckled and said, "I figured he'd see the light. Good for him. I imagine he'll come in handy in the Ward and Masek cases and maybe some others, but ol' lightning rod Weimar's been out of action for a long time."

Pointing to a seat, Kepner looked out the window and, in a nostalgic tone I'd never heard before said, "Ya know, Frank, it's kind of funny. It was Weimar who started this whole thing over six years ago when I was investigating him for bankruptcy fraud. He was nervous and hired Bob Bundy to explain the bankruptcy settlement and his side of some bogus valuations his creditors said cheated them out of the true value of the settlement. If I remember right he hid a bunch of assets and listed the value of his yacht at over a million dollars, but it only sold for a couple hundred thousand. We set up a meeting, listened to his pitch and let him think we were satisfied."

I thought for a moment and replied, "I remember getting a call from him sometime in 2002 or 2003 all relieved that you guys were off his back."

Kepner laughed, "Yeah, he's a creative guy and had his fingers in a lot of pies. I figured we'd get him on more than bankruptcy fraud, but I never dreamed how right you'd be when you said he would end up just one small fish in an ocean of sharks if we kept the investigation covert. Well, to everyone's surprise we kept this thing covert for nearly three years, that's gotta be some kind of record."

I smiled and said, "It's been a long haul, but you did good, girl."

Kepner paused, looked down for a moment, took a deep breath and replied, "Yeah, we sure did. Anyhow, I just need you to sign a couple of papers and the SAC wants to thank you for all you've done."

After I signed some forms, we stepped into the hallway and ran into U.S. Attorney Joe Bottini and Public Integrity Unit Prosecutor Nick Marsh. "Hey guys, how are ya?" I said. They both smiled, we exchanged a few words and they were off to a meeting. "Nice guys," I said. Kepner didn't answer as we walked down the hallway, cut through the glass wall conference atriums and headed for the SAC's office. Her silence and the long walk through familiar terrain pried open the floodgates of my mind releasing a surge of memories.

Kepner knocked on a mahogany door, it opened, she stepped to one side, and I walked into a room full of familiar smiling faces: special agents, federal prosecutors, technical staff, people I'd worked with closely over the past four years. I shook hands with a few and sat down. The SAC smiled and said, "Frank, every person in this room is here today to thank you." He was actually being quite literal (a common personality trait in the DOJ), so I sat for fifteen or so minutes enduring the attention, nodding, and smiling as people talked. I was both curious and touched by the surprise ceremony.

I think Nick Marsh was the last to speak. Then the room got quiet, everyone donned big grins and the SAC handed me a white box. I looked around the room as the grins morphed into suspicious Mona Lisa smiles. With a puzzled expression I lifted the lid, stared for a moment, and laughed as I pulled out a black, long-sleeve, button-down-collar shirt from JC Penney—without the wires. We shook hands again, I thanked everyone and blushed my way through the applause as Kepner escorted me back down the hall, through the atrium, down the stairs and into the security lobby. Kepner smiled, said she'd stay in touch and reached out to shake my hand. I ignored the official hand shake, gave her an awkward hug, stepped out onto the sidewalk and headed for my old Ford Bronco.

A split second later a female voice ricocheted off the concrete corridor and grazed my good ear, "Frank, I, uh--"

Without turning I paused, took a deep breath, raised my hand in a wave and continued down the sidewalk. Something had caught in my eye and I knew Confidential Sources weren't supposed to cry, it's right there in the manual.

Chapter Nine

Got Change?

Except for an occasional call asking this or that, I don't hear much from Kepner anymore, though we did catch up by phone in late July, 2008. She was in Washington DC and said things were looking pretty good with the investigations. That was a bit of an understatement considering U.S. Senator Ted Stevens was indicted on felony charges the next morning in a scheme to conceal gifts (including the $250,000 Girdwood house remodel) he received from VECO and Bill Allen over the course of their long, reciprocal, back-scratching friendship.

The last reliable word I heard from a pretty good source is that the Alaska corruption cases should wrap up by 2010 with a two percent margin of error on pleas or convictions of every name in this book, and a few more. Though four years in the making, I never really intended to make a lifetime work out of telling this story. I'm sure someone will write a scholarly treatise that will pass down as the definitive record of who, what, where, how, why, when, and the implications for global warming. Me? I just thought people might like to know how it all started from, well, a reliable source. My other reason for writing is more philosophical.

I grew up in Berkeley during the '50s and '60s and I've seen a lot of change over the years. There's change in the air these days. Political pundits in Alaska and Washington DC predict a "for better or worse" retirement (if not indictments) of senior U.S. Senator Ted Stevens and U.S. Congressman Don Young. Change recently occurred in our local elections as voters swept out the old right-leaning Anchorage Assembly in favor of a new left-leaning progressive majority. Recently Alaskans voted for change by electing a new, *transparent* governor to replace the Good Ol' Boy closed-door policies of the past. With little variation, this pattern is repeated every year in every community throughout our nation, it's called the democratic process.

Even as I write, national concern over war, hunger, housing, fuel prices, and climate change are shaping catalytic conditions for sweeping political change. Indeed, if we can be certain of one thing, it is that change happens, sometimes even for the good. The problem is that there are some fundamental things that never change and demand continuous and rigorous attention, if we are to foster and maintain a healthy environment.

It's historically predictable that Dante's men of Lucca would have hoisted a cold one to Ted Stevens, Don Young, Bill Allen, and the "git 'er done" *Divine Comedy* of Suite 604 regulars where still, 700 years later, *"del no, per li denar, visi fa ita"* (no, becomes yes, for money). And although the Machiavellian antics of Alaska's *we don't give a damn how they do it outside* politicians were bound to produce a unique frontier blend of Tuscan corruption, concern over violations of public trust are as old as the Babylonian and Hebraic codes from which the concerns spring.

From ancient Near East culture, Greek city states and the Roman Republic, to the Napoleonic Code and English Common Law, accepting money for personal gain in exchange for official acts (whether absolving sin, influencing judgment, or subverting an impartial public process) was a greater offense than a private act of violence. Rather than failure to restrain personal passion, violating public trust was considered a deep character flaw involving intellect and intent, which threatens the powerless. And by *powerless* they meant you and me and anyone else who relies on government for temporal peace, safety, and order.

In the wake of the Alaska corruption probe, there's been a lot of talk about the need for systemic change in the political process. Convinced that the corpus of state is terminally ill, talk radio, political blogs, editorial writers, political scientists, citizen initiatives and a new generation of nonprofit corporations compete in frenzied triage to diagnose and treat the electoral process, campaign finance law, special-interest influence, and ethics acts, all in a desperate national attempt to save us from ourselves. But when you step back (as we just have) and analyze political corruption case-by-case, the real disease appears neither systemic nor partisan. A dynamic and responsive government should continually fine-tune itself to serve public welfare in more efficient and effective ways and means. But whether the outcome benefits our common good, rather than a self-serving interest seems, in the final analysis, a matter of character…the individual character of the caretakers of public trust.

Yet, interestingly, in the national dialogue focus on personal character seems to have slipped from prominent to politically incorrect. When asked in recent times whether New York Governor Eliot Spitzer (*Time Magazine's* political corruption-fighting "Crusader of the Year") should step down after the FBI nabbed him in a wiretap and $2,000-per-hour tryst with an executive level hooker, famed Harvard Law School professor Alan Dershowitz opined, "Let's put this in perspective, it's a man and a prostitute. In most parts of the world it wouldn't even be a story. If every law-maker and law-enforcer who broke the law, even in a minor way, had to resign we'd have very few people in public office (CBS Evening News 03/10/08)." Oblivious of the implications, our philosopher rabbit would have smugly agreed with Dershowitz and raised the question, "Who are we to judge another animal's character?" to his pragmatic and salivating friend. What do *personal* values have to do with carrying out the *public* trust?

In a passing comment about lobbyists, former Speaker of the California House, Jesse Unruh said, "If you can't take their money, drink their whiskey, sleep with their women, and still look the bastards in the eye and vote against them, you don't belong in the legislature." Without knowing more about his personal character, my wife probably wouldn't have voted for Unruh on the basis of that quote, but he colorfully overstates my point. In a representative form of government, elected officials are supposed to be influenced by their constituents and other special and not-so-special interests affected by their legislation. It's ideas, not special interests, that threaten democracy, particularly the idea that right and wrong cannot be known and, therefore, cannot be used to guide and make demands upon the individual.

When each person or society is free to define right and wrong, rules for living become a moving target, continually changing under the influence of time and circumstance. With no basis in reality to judge right and wrong, the two become interchangeable and life becomes frighteningly unpredictable, until finally, when *my* right collides with *your* wrong, only the strong survive.

I read somewhere that genius is the ability to scrutinize the obvious. And it seems apparent that, try as they may, public officials cannot separate or compartmentalize their private selves from their public selves; people just don't change personal character like a pair of socks. If my neighbor lacks self-discipline, wisdom, and propriety in their personal life, why would I expect them to respond to public trust any differently? Patience, discipline, empathy, truthfulness, fair play, respect, and a long list of other achievable human qualities are (to resurrect another archaic notion) *virtues* that emanate from commitment and practice. To the observant or inquiring voter these virtues should be as apparent as the vices. But does it really matter?

Exemplary character doesn't guarantee success in public office and people of marginal character succeed, or at least maintain public office, all the time, particularly when surrounded by good people. After all, none of us is perfect. But a person who has earned a reputation for careless and undisciplined behavior, violating trust, self-indulgence, and twisting the truth will, if elected or appointed to public office, violate public trust. You can count on it. It's just who they are.

Decisions are driven by personal values, and personal values are apparent in the observed and observable daily life of every human being. In a representative form of government we are, or can become, close enough to local, state, and federal officials to know exactly who they are, *if it's important to us*. Integrity in government is not a matter of campaign finance reform, mandatory ethics training, or any other perceived systemic symptom or interest, it's a matter of character. Electing and appointing public officials with poor character will result in abuses of power that oppress the disenfranchised, unjustly enrich a privileged few, destabilize the economy, and undermine national security.

> Government is more than the sum of all the interests;
> it is the paramount interest, the public interest.
> It must be the efficient, effective agent of a responsible citizenry,
> not the shelter of the incompetent and the corrupt.
> *Adlai Stevenson*

In other words, character counts.

Conclusion

Navigating by air, land, or sea has an inherent complication: north on a compass rarely aligns with *true* north unless you're somewhere around Florida. Worse, the variation changes imperceptibly over the years. So in order to travel a true course one must take into account the attraction of the earth's magnetic field and adjust compass and heading. If you don't notice the variation and gradual deviation away from true north and correct course, the journey will end in disaster.

Life is much the same. Only 670,000 people live in Alaska and half live in Anchorage. Democracy is up-close and personal in a state where you can knock on the door to the governor's mansion or drop by your representative's house for a beer to air a beef or pitch an idea. I personally know most of the members of the Corrupt Bastards Club. Countless Alaskans have had years of legitimate interaction with the entire group. Bill Allen's list of charitable contributions is long. Bill Bobrick volunteered hundreds of hours helping programs for abused women. Ted Stevens and Don Young spent the lion's share of their political careers advocating and delivering funding and policy decisions that strengthened all of Alaska. And the same can be said for many of the others. I doubt that any started out their careers in public service or business with corrupt intent.

But over time the magnetic draw of money and power caused a gradual deviation in each moral compass, diverting them from the original course. With variations on theme, it happens to everyone. The difference is that most of us spot the deviance and quietly adjust heading, humbly thankful we avoided disaster and promising ourselves (and sometimes others) that we'll try to do better. Flush with power and lust for *the good life* the crew of the Corrupt Bastards Club partied through the night, failing to compensate for the deviation that placed their vessel on direct heading with the shallow water, jagged rocks, and pounding surf under the last bridge to nowhere.

Acknowledgements

A book like this can't be written without the intentional and unintentional contributions of a huge cast of players. Topping the list is my wife and best friend, Vicki. Without her love, trust, and support I doubt that I could have sustained the creative energy and stamina to both write and serve as the government's chief source. It was a marathon and she finished well. I am eternally grateful for her love.

I was deeply touched and thankful that my perceived *radioactivity* only stimulated my friends and family to circle my flanks like a herd of musk ox protecting one of their own, though I would not have expected otherwise. I also thank authors Dallas Willard, Phillip Yancey, and Eugene H. Peterson for decades of mentoring that contributed greatly to my ability to trust God when the going really got tough; and William J. Bennett, whose remarks at the 2000 National Symposium on *Character in Politics* helped to shape my own thoughts on the subject.

A special word of thanks to the *Anchorage Daily News* team of journalists who have tirelessly covered the events chronicled herein and helped fill in pieces to the puzzle that even many who were closer to the events missed: Sabra Ayres, Erika Bolstad, Sean Cockerham, Lisa Demer, Kyle Hopkins, Tom Kizzia, Wesley Loy, and Richard Mauer. Likewise Chuck Neubauer and Richard T. Cooper of the *Los Angeles Times,* whose 2003 springboard investigative journalism pried open closed doors.

And, of course, the United States Department of Justice. The agents, attorneys, and staff I worked with make me proud to be an American.

The integrity, dedication, self-sacrifice I witnessed gives me confidence that even in our national disagreements the United States can remain a stronghold and protector of freedom and human rights. Thank you Mary Beth, Chad, Nick, Joe, and staff.

Special Agent Kepner told me a lot of people were pretty upset when word leaked that I was writing a book about the Alaska political corruption scandal. Evidently they were mostly people who wanted the inside track on writing *the book*. A few bloggers were particularly indignant that the "slime-ball" lobbyist who cut a deal with the Feds would have the audacity to capitalize on "blood money" proceeds from a book. Though it's never fun to be a target, people do have a right to be angry. Violations of public trust *and* knee-jerk prejudgment are painful gifts that keep on giving. The high road lies in responsibly managing the pain and it's my hope this book will help dispense a bit of grace between neighbors.

And finally, to all the prospective authors who somehow feel shortchanged by my preemptive publication, I sincerely hope this book serves as a foundation and catalyst for a more definitive work by a thoughtful, research-diligent, unbiased source. A historic event of this stature deserves no less.

Author's Retrospective

Remember when I wrote about sitting on a mountaintop overlooking Anchorage and wondering, "Why me?" As you can imagine, being a pivotal player in a drama of this magnitude evokes a bit of existential reflection. The body of the story was neither the time nor place to deal with such matters, but some readers may be interested in the personal experiences that influenced and, in my opinion, guided the outcome of events.

You see, I believe in divine power. For lack of a more precise definition, we'll call the power God. Worse than that, I actually believe God is an active participant in life. Now some people get stuck on the idea of God. I actually think that's okay with God, who, in my estimation, just wants us to be intellectually honest enough to wrestle with the notion that he (she, if you prefer) may actually exist and want a relationship with the people he created after his own image. Who wouldn't? The choice to believe, of course, belongs to you, not God. So you could say God is pro-choice and progressive, notwithstanding his pro-life reputation. If you're already settled that God doesn't exist, or has no interest in human events, then you'll probably have little interest in the rest of my story. But before you go, thank you for your time and I sincerely hope this book has provoked some critical thinking and a couple of chuckles between the lines of political irreverence.

Speaking of irreverence, some readers may have been uncomfortable considering serious moral and public policy issues in the rather coarse cloak of contemporary satire. I struggled a bit with the concern and sincerely mean no offense, especially to the unfortunate souls who are caught on the stage of the real-life drama. When C.S. Lewis was questioned about the propriety of mixing "a light touch" with heavy moral themes, he defended the integration of "buffoonery" and "farce" as a literary device commonly used by classic writers to relate truth to the everyday human experience. I can think of no finer description of the antics of the Corrupt Bastards Club than *buffoonery* and *farce*. And although I'm no C.S. Lewis, without moral context this tragic tale would merely be twisted situation comedy, and rather poor comedy at that.

Okay, back to God. I don't know about you, but the older I get the more skeptical I become of politicians, priests, preachers, professors, promoters, programmers, protesters and proctologists. It seems to me the great irony of the *information age* is that the more we receive the less we trust; the less we trust the more isolated we become; the more isolated we become the more vulnerable we are; the more vulnerable we are the greater our risk; the greater the risk the more probable the harm; and when life's inevitable harms occur, the less equipped we are to cope. There was a time when lies were lies rather than savvy marketing, crafty campaigning, and clever strategy. These days it just seems harder to know who and what we can trust.

But as Alexander Pope observed, *hope springs eternal in the human breast.* So we move through the pain and disappointments thinking the next election might reduce crime, curb global warming, promote world peace, balance the budget, and bring *"yes-we-can"* change; or deregulating human embryo research will eliminate disease and prolong life; or a pay raise, equity loan, reverse mortgage, stock tip, or lottery win will move us from anxiety to a place of personal peace and prosperity. As long as that's the kind of *hope* that springs from the human breast, there's little incentive to explore a life of faith outside ourselves. Convinced that our immediate challenges or experiences are unique, most of us spend our entire lives trying to escape, modify, and influence what life does, or threatens to do to us. But poverty, rape, war, political corruption, bankruptcy, broken relationships, tough breaks, disease, and opportunism just don't seem to go away.

Belief in God doesn't inoculate us from the natural consequences of life any more than my neighbor's frenzied defensive efforts to avoid life's pits and potholes. As a crudely poignant bumper sticker once declared, *"shit happens."* In the ups and downs of life I find God a bit like a navigation aid. Anyone who has hiked, sailed, or navigated the streets of any major city understands the value of a map and GPS. A map shows you where you've been and where you're heading; a global positioning system shows you where you are. A relationship with God helps make sense out of where you've been, where you're going and pinpoints with naked precision, exactly where you are. Better than that, in addition to navigational aid God is a loving, reliable companion and experienced guide. The result? Given similar life events, people who believe and cultivate a relationship with God statistically live longer, happier, healthier, less anxious and more purposeful lives, and that's just in this lifetime.

So what's not to like about God? I'm afraid the answer is quite simple. He's in charge and he wants us to trust him, and trust just doesn't come easy, particularly when it means surrendering freedom of choice. Afraid that God was an *occupying*, rather than *liberating* force, C.S. Lewis once exclaimed, "I was dragged kicking and screaming into the Kingdom of God, eyes darting left and right for some means of escape." But after taking a look around, Lewis realized he'd never known real freedom until he came to know God. You see, trust isn't about surrendering free will, it's about embracing and relaxing in God's will. The divine irony is we are all free to choose to live and move within the narrow confines of our own will, or step into the *freedom-without-borders* of his. Freedom of choice and personal freedom are two different concerns.

U.S.C. Philosophy Professor Dallas Willard observes, "What we do or do not understand, in any area of our lives, determines what we can or cannot believe and therefore governs our practice and action with an iron hand." I don't know whether divine intervention, my poor choices or a combination of these caused my lifeline to intersect with the FBI. But I do know it isn't the first time I've entrusted God with the bitter lemons in my life and he made killer margaritas.

The week the FBI came knocking I was finishing Willard's book, *Hearing God* (the quote above is on page 190). Willard convincingly argues that God's greatest desire is to walk in conversational relationship with his creation. And while he rarely imposes himself on us, Willard says God will respond to our sincere and loving desire to communicate with him. His responses may not always fit our paradigms but, like in any relationship, the more time you spend together the better you communicate.

The morning of April 20, 2004 was no different than most mornings. I usually try to spend a little time reading the Bible, something thought-provoking, or just sit and reflect for a few minutes. Like any good friendship, I believe a relationship with God is a two-way proposition rather than a spectator sport. So I ask God to actively participate in my day, including speaking to me and directing me in ways I can see, hear, and understand. But mostly I just want God to enjoy being with me, exactly the way I feel about my wife and other people I love. I then expectantly greet the day as containing something bigger than me in which I am privileged to participate. A few hours later the FBI showed up with a wonderful plan for my life.

After a restless night's sleep I got up around six a.m., made coffee, opened the door, looked at the dog and said, "Emmy, pee and paper!" Which for the modest price of one *Yummy Chummy*, she enthusiastically complied with on both counts. A bit distracted and finding little of interest, I was about to put the paper down when I noticed my daily horoscope. I'm not really into horoscopes, but I was pleased to note that I was going to have a five-star day advising, "You might want to play a situation cool, but cannot despite what is happening. You might say too much or reveal more than necessary. Learn to muzzle yourself sometimes. Take your time rather than jumping in." Well, under the circumstances that seemed like pretty prudent advice, so I walked to my office to ask God for his.

I had been enjoying an unusual translation of the Bible called *The Message* and told God I could sure use some guidance. I had been reading a New Testament book called *Matthew* and opened to chapter 10 where I had left off a day or two before. The chapter is about Jesus telling twelve of his disciples to travel around and heal sick people, toss out evil spirits, and stir up attention about his new political movement. But as I read, the text transformed from its historical context into what felt like a heart-penetrating personal letter:

> Stay alert. This is hazardous work I'm assigning you. You're going to be like sheep running through a wolf pack. Be as cunning as a snake and inoffensive as a dove.

> Don't be naïve. Some people will impugn your motives, others will smear your reputation---just because you believe in

me. Don't be upset when they haul you before the authorities. Without knowing it they've done you—and me—a favor, given you a platform for preaching the Kingdom news. And don't worry about what you'll say or how you'll say it. The right words will be there; the Spirit of your Father will supply the words.

Don't be intimidated. Eventually everything is going to be out in the open, and everyone will know how things really are. So don't hesitate to go public now. Don't be bluffed into silence by the threats of bullies. There's nothing they can do to your soul, your core being. Save your fear for God, who holds your entire life, body and soul, in his hands.

What's the price of a canary? Some loose change, right? And God cares what happens to it even more than you do. He pays even greater attention to you, down to the last detail. So don't be intimidated by this bully talk. Stand up for me against world opinion and I'll stand up for you.
Matthew 10: 16-35

I thought, "Well, what will it be, the Horoscope or the Bible?" Now I suppose God is perfectly capable of speaking through both, but I put my money on the Bible. I read the words over and over and even smiled at the *canary* reference because in the James Cagney sense, that's exactly what I was being asked to be, and we all know how much everyone loves a snitch. As I reflected on the words the name of a person I hadn't seen or spoken with in ten or fifteen years came to mind, so I picked up the phone book to see if he was still around. Mike Spaan is a former U.S. Attorney who camouflages his sharp legal mind in a good ol' boy spring-trap that leaves unwary opponents swinging upside down in front of admiring judge and jurors. I served on a couple of committees with him, enjoyed his wit, shared an occasional beer, and dropped by his closing arguments once in a while for sport. I found his name associated with the prestigious Patton Boggs law firm and dialed.

A receptionist answered and transferred me to Mike's secretary who put me on hold. A few seconds later I was relieved to hear the familiar drawl of a voice from my past. We exchanged "how ya beens," I gave him the Cliffs Notes version of my predicament and he amazingly cleared his calendar for the following afternoon. I put down the phone, took a deep breath and, for reasons I cannot begin to explain (because I rarely read the Hebrew prophets) sensed that I should read the second chapter of Micah. Now I love trying to listen to God, and I suspect I dismiss his voice as my thoughts or mere coincidence more often than not, but I about fell over when I read Micah's warning:

> Doom to those who plot evil, who go to bed dreaming up crimes. As soon as it's morning they're off, full of energy, doing what they've planned. They covet fields and grab them. They bully the neighbor and his family, see people only for what they can get out of them.

> God has had enough! He says, "I have some plans of my own: disaster because of the interbreeding of evil. Your necks are on the line. You're not walking away from this. It's doomsday for you. Mocking ballads will be sung of you and you yourselves will sing the blues: our lives are ruined, our homes and land auctioned off, all sold to the highest bidder. And there will be no one to stand up for you, no one to speak for you before God and his jury.

I was speechless. At the time I didn't know the full extent of the names that would eventually end up on the Alaska Political Corruption hit list. But as it turned out, all the names matched some or all of the character, issues, and attitudes God was fed up with a few thousand years earlier in a different time and place. Interestingly, after the first round of indictments *mocking songs* actually started popping up on U-Tube, local news, and a variety of websites with ballads to the Corrupt Bastards Club; many of the defendants went on record proclaiming financial and professional ruin; the VECO CEO said his life was about over; and the multimillion-dollar family-owned company was sold to the highest bidder.

The morning of April 22 I spent preparing for my afternoon appointment with Spann. Concentration was a bit difficult because, well, I was scared spitless. I took a deep breath, apologized for my lack of faith, reminded God that he knew my heart and asked him to protect me from the false accusations I had heard. For no particular reason other than a desire to communicate, I turned to the last paragraph of Ecclesiastes 2 which bluntly says, *Fear God. Do what he tells you. And that's it. Eventually God will bring everything that we do out into the open and judge it according to its hidden intent, whether it's good or evil.* Well, that seemed clear enough, so I said, "okay," and got ready for my meeting.

That afternoon I laid out the story to Mike. He listened carefully, said he thought he could be helpful, picked up the phone and arranged a meeting with the FBI and U.S. Attorneys for the following afternoon. They, of course, had been expecting the call. The next morning I committed the day to God in my usual manner and asked if there were any specific instructions or guidance because, frankly, the dose of encouragement from the day before had worn off and I was pretty nervous, again. I was wearing a pair of slacks that I'd worn to a church service several weeks before and for some reason reached into a pocket and felt a small, one-by-two-inch red satin ribbon that had been handed out during communion to remind us of God's sacrificial love. I had no idea the ribbon was there, but the timely reminder was pretty amazing. I took a deep breath (I seemed to be doing a lot of deep breathing that week), my eyes filled with tears, I mumbled "thanks" (or some equally pathetic understatement), and followed a compelling sense that I should open my Bible to Ephesians 3 where the Apostle Paul writes:

> When we trust in him, we're free to say whatever needs to be said, bold to go wherever we need to go. Reach out and experience the breadth. Test its length. Plumb the depths. Rise to the heights. Live full lives, full in the fullness of God. God can do anything, you know—far more than you could ever imagine or guess or request in your wildest dreams! He does it not by pushing us around but by working within us, his Spirit deeply and gently within us.

With those encouraging words drifting through my mind, I stepped into my old Bronco, fired up the engine and jumped out of my skin! The previous evening I had loaded the back of the truck with trash, cranked the ignition and *turned off* the blaring radio so I could have some quiet time at the end of the driveway with my garbage. When I started her up the next morning I lunged for the volume control as an excruciating, eardrum-bursting song filled the universe. As I punched the volume down I recognized a song from a CD I keep over the visor above my head. I looked up and, sure enough, it was gone. The song (now within hearing range) is seven tracks into the CD and entitled *Refiners Fire*. It goes like this:

> Purify my heart Lord,
> Let me be as gold and precious silver.
> Purify my heart Lord,
> Let me be as gold, pure gold.
> Refiner's fire
> My heart's one desire is to be holy
> Set apart for you Lord.
> I choose to be holy
> Set apart for you my master
> Ready to do your will.

Who says God doesn't have a sense of humor? For the skeptics, I concede that I can't prove God swiped the CD and turned on the stereo just to get my attention, and I doubt he leaves fingerprints or DNA. I also can't prove he actually speaks or directs in the manner I have earlier suggested. But I like the odds, particularly when my hand is entirely played out (which, I suspect, is exactly when most people find time for God). I guess I think that's what faith is all about. Besides, God probably doesn't need me to prove he exists. So I listened to the song several times on my drive to the Federal Building and it kind of became my mantra over the next couple of years (God's okay with *mantras* as long as they're aimed in his direction). The words were evidently something he wanted me to think about. And, like I said, I try to listen and comply as much as possible.

I entered the interrogation room at two p.m. on April 23, 2004 and was greeted by a skeptical, suspicious crowd of federal agents who had obvious preconceived notions that I, or my clients, had been involved in an elaborate RICO racketeering scheme to defraud the State of Alaska. Over two days of meetings the emotional atmosphere in the room warmed, trust developed, the agenda shifted, and the cast for the first act of the Alaska Political Follies was set when Special Agent Kepner said, "Frank, would you be willing to help us?" Of course, by that time

I suspected Kepner had a cosmic partner, whether she knew it or liked it or not. So who was I to argue over the terms of the contract?

I came home at the end of the second day exhausted. I told my wife I needed a minute, went to my office, sat down in my old chair, picked up my Bible and said, "Okay God, are you done yet?" Well, I guess he wasn't, because I had no idea why I was turning to Psalm 18 other than to see what else he had to say:

> But me he caught…reached all the way from sky to sea; he pulled me out of that ocean of hate, that enemy chaos, the void in which I was drowning. They hit me when I was down, but God stuck by me. He stood me up on a wide-open field. I stood there saved, surprised to be loved! God made my life complete when I placed all the pieces before him. When I got my act together he gave me a fresh start. Now I'm alert to God's ways. I don't take God for granted. Every day I review the ways he works; I try not to miss a trick. I feel put back together and I'm watching my step. God rewrote the text of my life when I opened the book of my heart to his eyes.

As the investigations kicked into gear I craved God's guidance and trusted he was leading, but as far as I could tell he stopped speaking directly to me in such explicit, relevant, and timely detail until three years later at the Anderson trial. As I explained earlier, no one expected Tom Anderson to plead not guilty. But everyone knew that if he did, the only way the defense could sway the jury was to twist the truth, impugn my character, and destroy my credibility with the jury. Not a very nice strategy and my mother would have disapproved (my mother, incidentally, died during the trial and knowing her, *Frankie's* well-being was her first point of business on the other side). All the defense needed to do was create a reasonable doubt in one juror's mind to win an acquittal. So I was immensely relieved the day before I was scheduled to testify when God finally spoke again through another unlikely source, a guy named Jeremiah who (like I said before) I rarely read. In Jeremiah 42 God said:

> I feel deep compassion on account of the doom I have visited on you. You don't have to fear the King of Babylon. Your fears

are for nothing. I'm on your side ready to save and deliver you from anything he might do. I'll pour mercy on you.

In prophetic literature some scholars argue that the King of Babylon is Satan. So I was pleased to be forewarned that there was nothing personal about the attack; some of the critics may have just been acting under boss's orders. After Anderson was convicted on *all* seven counts my phone rang. It was Marc June, a highly respected Anchorage attorney who said, "Frank, so much for your lack of credibility. I heard the result. Great job!" I thanked him, hung up, looked up and said, "Yeah God, great job."

And the rest is going down in history as I write.

Sure, there was some twisted press coverage, uninformed blogs, and a nasty editorial, but as you recall God warned me from the outset that, *some people will impugn your motives, others will smear your reputation…don't be upset…without knowing it they've given you a platform for preaching the Kingdom news (Matt 10)*. I have to confess I did get pretty upset a couple times. But God seems to handle my imperfection pretty well, at least a whole lot better than the people around me, though that probably has something to do with *their* own imperfection. You see I think that God really loves people, all kinds of people. It doesn't matter who we are or what we've done. Like any good father, he just wants the best for us and I'm privileged he entrusted me with a platform to honor him, in spite of my shortcomings.

I haven't heard much from God directly over the past few months. Maybe it's because I talk too much. Or maybe it's because he's kept me too busy to get into more trouble. But we have a great time together and I've given him carte blanche to grab my attention anytime he needs to. I also told Kepner the next time she needs help, "*PLEASE*, just ask."

———·———

I look up to the mountains.
Does my strength come from mountains?
No, my strength comes from God,
who made heaven, and earth, and mountains.
He won't let you stumble,
your guardian God won't fall asleep.

Not on your life!
Israel's Guardian will never doze or sleep.
God is your Guardian,
right at your side to protect you—
shielding you from sunstroke,
sheltering you from moonstroke.
God guards you from every evil,
He guards your very life.
He guards you when you leave and when you return,
He guards you now, He guards you always.
Psalm 121

Glossary of Alaska Terms and Phrases

Alaska Tuxedo - An old, green, out-of-style Filson wool coat, vest, and pants

Alcan - The Alaska-Canada highway connecting Alaska to anywhere "outside"

ANWR - Arctic National Wildlife Refuge. Environmentalists' holy mantra until polar bear are classified endangered

Arctic Entry - An enclosed, odiferous, catch-all porch that allows the exterior door to close against frigid arctic blasts of air before the interior door is opened

Aurora Borealis aka Northern Lights A colorful, dancing display of solar energy that romances up Alaska's long winter nights

Baleen - Fringed, black, flexible bone-like rows in a whale's mouth that catch small sea creatures before they (the baleen, not the creatures) adorn Alaska walls as Indigenous Art

Bear Repellent - The ability to run faster than your fishing or hiking partner

Beaver Fever - A debilitating intestinal bug you catch drinking from freshwater streams that beavers and other creatures use for a variety of disgusting but natural purposes

Blazo - A liquid fuel

Blazo Box - Wooden box that holds two cans of Blazo and doubles as kitchen cabinet

Bootie - Colorful fabric footwear for pampered sled dogs

Bottom Fishing - 1. Taunting creatures who inhabit the ocean floor to bite a hook and fight real hard before joining the food chain 2. FBI political corruption investigation

Borough - Alaska equivalent of a county unless you live in Anchorage *Municipality*

Bore - 1. A single wave known as a Tidal Bore that provides thrills to beluga whale, hooligan, surfers, kayakers, geezers and gawkers along Turnagain Arm between Anchorage and Girdwood 2. A date for lunch at Costco

Breakup - Alaska equivalent of spring when things covered by snow surface, thaw and smell terrible

Bunny Boots - Balloon-like white rubber boots designed by the U.S. Army for extreme cold and public humiliation

Bush - Small rural Alaska villages that appear as a speck from the air after a two-hour flight from anywhere

Bush Pilot - A person who makes a living defying death by taking people to and from the Bush to hunt, fish, etc.

Butte - The backside of Palmer, Alaska, a city north of Anchorage

CBC - The designation on caps made for the Corrupt Bastards Club of Alaska legislators and an extinct oil service company

Cabin Fever - A mid-season excursion to the dark side brought on by long, cold winter days and nights stuffing carbs and watching tv

Cache - Little cabin-like shed on tall legs that keeps big and little critters out of whatever one decides to store in the shed - doubles as a winter deep freeze - smells real bad at *Breakup* (see above)

Chain - A chain of islands known as the Aleutians that stretches from Alaska to Asia and hosts extreme fishing and crabbing industries in the Bering Sea

Cheechacko - New immigrant to Alaska who hasn't yet survived one full winter

Combat Fishing - A peculiar annual ritual that sorts the weak from the strong. At the same time every year, fishermen (and women) gather shoulder to shoulder casting a gauntlet of nylon line, lead weight, and sharp hooks in hope of catching passing salmon. Until the thinning process is complete, mystified salmon pause in transit to watch fishermen hook vital body parts, knock each other silly with lead weights, and lacerate exposed flesh in pole-slamming, nylon-line-whipping frenzy. The actual catching of fish occurs only after natural selection has balanced the competitive order.

Cross The Gulf - Travel by boat from Southcentral to Southeast Alaska across the Gulf of Alaska…an impressive and usually unforgettable experience

Dip Netting - An alternative to Combat Fishing where fishermen and women wade into the water and sweep long-handled nets along the riverbed hoping an unsuspecting salmon will swim into the net

Deet - The active ingredient in a variety of concoctions that promise immunity from mosquitoes. The higher the Deet percentage the lower the number of bites

Duct Tape - A versatile product Alaskans use to patch, seal, mend, repair, and adorn just about anything e.g. "Dear, when I want your opinion I'll remove the duct tape."

Ditch Divers - Vehicles stuck and scattered in medians and shoulders along Alaska highways and roads after a snowstorm

Fourwheeler - Preferred mode of summer transportation in Bush Alaska

Fourwheelin' - Taking your life in your hands riding a Fourwheeler through the Bush

Freeze-up - The short period of time between summer and winter when the trees are naked, the grass is brown, and the ground takes on the character of concrete

Frost Heave - Huge bumps in the highway caused by freezing and thawing that catapult a vehicle like a giant bullfrog if care isn't taken to drive attentively

Gangline - A rope or chain running down the center of a dog team to which each is attached and which is no longer allowed to secure prisoners

Greenie - One of the more polite Alaska terms used to describe an environmentalist

Green-up - A designation of time e.g. "I'll be back in Spring after things 'green up' a bit"

Head-bolt Heater - A plug-in device that warms an engine by heating oil or percolating warm coolant through the system a couple of hours before you crank her over.

Honey Bucket - A five gallon bucket used as a toilet in the Bush where there is no plumbing and it's too cold for an outhouse. The contents are stored in a larger container outside and left to freeze until breakup, when it's hauled off (before it thaws, hopefully)

Hooligan - A lot like smelt. Arctic peoples also call them Candle Fish because the oil will burn like a candle, an acquired taste and odor

Ice Fog - A freezing fog that coats trees, bushes and power lines with beautiful ice crystals until they collapse from the weight

Ice Worm - Tiny worms that live on and in glaciers at or near freezing temperature (I'm serious)

Iditarod - The annual sled dog race from Anchorage to Nome run in memory of serum that was conveyed from Anchorage to Nome during a 1925 outbreak of diphtheria

Inside Passage - The sailing route from roughly Juneau to Seattle allowing vessels to travel through protected fjords rather than the North Pacific Ocean

Kenai - The Kenai River runs through the city of Kenai and hosts world-class salmon fishing, including *Combat Fishing* noted above

Lower 48 - Where other Americans live, you know, *outside* (see below)

Marine Highway - Alaska ferry system that connects communities along the Inside Passage, Prince William Sound, Seward, and Kodiak

McKinley - What most Alaskans over 30 call Denali

Midnight Sun - A large, bright object in the sky that enables Alaskans to play softball, fish, and hike in the middle of the night during the summer

Mosquito - A voracious airborne bloodsucker that pesters people taking advantage of the midnight sun

Mukluk – A traditional seal-skin and fur, mid-calf boot that is lighter, as warm, and more aesthetically pleasing to the eye than the military Bunny Boot

Muktuk - Cubes or strips of whale fat with skin, an hors d'oeuvre de la preference to Alaskan Eskimos, an acquired taste for others

No-See-Um – Misnomer for the vicious ceratopogonidae flying fangs that rip chunks of flesh from exposed body parts and leave welts the size of a golf ball

Nugget - 1. Moose poop (really) 2. A large chunk of gold in its natural state that Alaskans carry in a pocket, wear on a wrist watch, or hang from a neck

Oosik - The penis bone of a walrus, usually fifteen to thirty inches. Polished and scrimshawed, oosiks adorn the mantels and desktops of people with twisted sense of art and humor.

Outside - Where Alaskans travel and everyone else is from

PFD - Alaska Permanent Fund rainy-day savings account that produces an annual check for one or two thousand dollars for every Alaskan. A popular deterrent to birth control for some groups of homo sapien stupidous

Permafrost - Permanently frozen ground that causes problems for anything above if it melts: note *Frost Heaves*, above

Qiviut - A downy feeling under-fur of Musk Ox that is woven into soft, warm, and very expensive accessories

Scrub Spruce - A pathetic, undernourished spruce that grows in peat bogs

Skookum - An Indian expression ordinarily used to describe something that is structurally sound, well-designed, or just plain cool

Snagging - Intentionally or unintentionally hooking a fish anywhere except the mouth

Sourdough - Anyone who has lived in Alaska long enough to call a newcomer a *Cheechacko* (above)

Spenard Divorce - Ending a live-in relationship with a shotgun and a shot of whiskey

Spit - The strip of land that juts into Kachemak Bay from Homer, Alaska, featuring the famed Salty Dawg Saloon and world-class halibut charters.

Studrut – 1. Two parallel grooves within one lane of a road caused by winter studs wearing through asphalt, a pleasure to navigate. 2. Alaska male mating ritual performed on Friday night in most Anchorage bars.

Summer - An semi-annual event that usually occurs around July

Termination Dust - The first snowfall that sticks on the mountain tops, terminating all summer fun and signaling a massive list of prewinter honey-do's

The Third Floor - A colloquialism for the Alaska governor's office or the governor's opinions e.g. "Have you heard from the third floor?"

Ulu - An Eskimo skinning and chopping knife with a half-moon curved blade and handle on top

Valley Trash - A former, soon-to-be-indicted Alaska senator's reference to people who live an hour north of Anchorage in the Mat-Su Valley.

Whitekeys - A guy who used to perform Alaska political parodies at the *Spenard* (above) Fly By Night Club

Whiteknuckle - The state of most travelers' hands when they land at most Alaska airports

Winter King - An Alaska King (Chinook) Salmon with white meat and extraordinary Omega 3 content usually caught trolling during the winter in the deep waters of the Inside Passage and North Gulf Coast of Alaska - *deeeeliciousss!*

Zapper - A tennis-racket device that zaps mosquitoes with an electric current and serves as cheap entertainment at parties featuring beer and shots

Frank Prewitt has lived in Alaska for thirty five years and served as an Assistant Attorney General, Deputy Commissioner and Commissioner under Alaska Governors Bill Sheffield, Steve Cowper, and Walter Hickel. In 1995 Frank left state service and opened a

government affairs consulting and lobbying practice. A familiar face in Alaska political circles, Frank was *recruited* by the FBI because of his systemic knowledge and inside access to persons-of-interest to the Government. From 2004 to 2007 Frank worked covert undercover investigations as an FBI Confidential Source exposing Alaska's sub-culture of political corruption. Under code name Patient, Frank provided indispensable strategic consultation, covert operations and trial testimony that laid the foundation for the continuing investigation and indictments that followed.